THE 39 CLUES

ONE FALSE NOTE

THE 39 CLUES

ONE FALSE NOTE

BY GORDON KORMAN

A GRAPHIC NOVEL BY

HANNAH TEMPLER

WITH COLOR BY GEORGE WILLAMS

graphix

AN IMPRINT OF

SCHOLASTIC

Library of Congress Control Number: 2024003755

ISBN 978-93-5954-927-9

This reprint edition, January 2025

Edited by Mallory Kass
Lettering by Joamette Gil
Book design by Carina Taylor
Creative Director: Phil Falco
Publisher: David Saylor

Printed in India at MicroPrints India, New Delhi

For all the brother-sister teams, from the Mozarts through the Cahills, from a grateful only child.

—GK

For all the little brothers who egg their big sisters on.

—HT

ONE

THE HUNGER STRIKE BEGAN TWO HOURS EAST OF PARIS.
COME ON, SALADIN. HERE'S YOUR DINNER.
IT'S FISH! REAL TUNA!
COME ON... WON'T YOU AT LEAST *TRY* IT? YOU HAVE TO EAT ***SOMETHING.***
HMPH
SHE'S RIGHT, CAT. IT'S A LONG WAY TO VIENNA.

I'M SORRY... I THINK HE'S JUST USED TO RED SNAPPER. THAT'S WHAT GRACE WOULD FEED HIM.
WHAT?! HE EATS BETTER THAN I DO!
MRRP.
DO YOU HAVE ANY IDEA HOW MUCH FRESH FISH COSTS? WE'VE GOT TO MAKE OUR MONEY LAST. WHO KNOWS HOW LONG WE'LL BE RUNNING AROUND LOOKING FOR THESE PRECIOUS CLUES OF YOURS?
AT THIS RATE, ***FOREVER***. I CAN'T BELIEVE WE HAD TO TAKE THE SLOWEST TRAIN IN EUROPE.
I MEAN, THE COMPETITION HAS ***PRIVATE JETS,*** AND WE'RE WASTING TIME ON THE LOSER EXPRESS.
ARE WE GOING TO STOP IN EVERY PODUNK TOWN IN FRANCE?

NO. PRETTY SOON IT'LL STOP IN EVERY PODUNK TOWN IN GERMANY. THEN EVERY PODUNK TOWN IN AUSTRIA.
LOOK, IT WAS CHEAP, OKAY? I DIDN'T AGREE TO BABYSIT YOU GUYS ON THIS QUEST --
AU PAIR US ON THE QUEST.
-- JUST TO HAVE YOU DROP OUT HALFWAY THROUGH BECAUSE YOU BLEW ALL YOUR CASH ON SNAPPER AND EXPENSIVE TRAIN TICKETS!
WE REALLY APPRECIATE YOUR HELP, NELLIE. WE COULD NEVER DO THIS WITHOUT YOU.

AMY AND DAN WERE STILL DIZZY FROM THE WHIRLWIND OF THE PAST TWO WEEKS. ONE MINUTE, THEY'D BEEN ORPHANS. THE NEXT, THEY WERE PART OF THE MOST POWERFUL FAMILY THE WORLD HAD EVER KNOWN.
SOME OF THE MOST INFLUENTIAL PEOPLE IN HISTORY HAD BEEN CAHILLS: BENJAMIN FRANKLIN, WOLFGANG AMADEUS MOZART, AND MORE -- GENIUSES, VISIONARIES, AND GLOBAL LEADERS.
OVER THE CENTURIES, THE FAMILY'S POWER HAD BEEN LOST -- SCATTERED AROUND THE WORLD IN THE FORM OF THIRTY-NINE CLUES. THE FIRST TO ASSEMBLE THE CLUES WOULD BECOME THE MOST POWERFUL CAHILL OF ALL.

THEIR GRANDMOTHER GRACE HAD SET UP THE CONTEST IN HER WILL. AMY STILL DIDN'T FULLY UNDERSTAND WHY GRACE HAD WANTED HER AND DAN TO PARTICIPATE. THEY WERE JUST KIDS! HOW COULD THEY KEEP UP WITH THEIR WEALTHY RIVALS?
THEIR RELATIVES WOULD STOP AT ***NOTHING*** TO DEFEAT THEM. WITH ULTIMATE POWER HANGING IN THE BALANCE, THE DEATHS OF TWO AMERICAN ORPHANS WOULD BE BARELY A FOOTNOTE...
BUT THEY COULDN'T GIVE UP NOW. AFTER ALL, THEY HAD ***ALREADY FOUND*** THE FIRST CLUE, AFTER A TREACHEROUS OBSTACLE COURSE THROUGH THE LIFE OF BENJAMIN FRANKLIN.
THEY WERE CONVINCED THAT MOZART WAS THE KEY TO THE SECOND. THE ANSWER LAY AT THE END OF THESE RAILROAD TRACKS IN VIENNA, WHERE MOZART HAD LIVED AND COMPOSED SOME OF THE GREATEST MUSIC OF ALL TIME.
THEY COULD ONLY HOPE THAT THE COMPETITION WOULDN'T GET THERE FIRST.

I HATE FRANCE. THIS HAMBURGER IS SO TINY!
YEAH! AND THERE'S WAY TOO MUCH MUSTARD.
IT'S **DIJON,** STUPID. THIS IS THE MUSTARD CAPITAL OF THE WORLD.
GARE DE DIJON-VILLE
EYES ON THE PRIZE, HOLTS. WHEN WE FIND THE THIRTY-NINE CLUES, WE CAN KISS THESE STARVATION RATIONS GOODBYE AND HIT SOME ALL-YOU-CAN-EAT BUFFETS BACK IN THE STATES...
BUT FOR NOW, WE'VE GOT TO CATCH UP WITH THOSE CAHILL BRATS. EVERYONE READY?
SIR, YES, SIR!
-VILLE
OKAY -- FORMATION!
SKREEE

ANY LUCK?
ZILCH. ARE YOU SURE THIS MOZART DUDE WAS A CAHILL? I MEAN, BEN FRANKLIN HARDLY BLEW HIS NOSE WITHOUT PLANTING A CODED MESSAGE IN THE KLEENEX. THIS IS NOTHING BUT BORING MUSIC.
CRONCH
"THIS MOZART DUDE"? WERE YOU **BORN** A DOOFUS, OR DID YOU HAVE TO GET A DIPLOMA? WOLFGANG AMADEUS MOZART IS CONSIDERED THE GREATEST CLASSICAL COMPOSER WHO EVER LIVED.
RIGHT, CLASSICAL. BORING.
STOP THAT, SALADIN. DAN, MUSICAL NOTES CORRESPOND TO THE LETTERS A THROUGH G. MAYBE THERE'S A HIDDEN MESSAGE?
BEEN THERE, DONE THAT. I EVEN TRIED UNSCRAMBLING THE LETTERS IN CASE THE WORDS WERE ANAGRAMS. FACE IT -- WE ALMOST GOT KILLED FOR A CLUE THAT ISN'T REALLY A CLUE.
IT'S A CLUE. IT HAS TO BE...
CLANG
SQUAWK SQUAWK

OH NO... THE HO-- HO--
HOLTS!!
COME ON, LADY --
SQUAWK
SQUAWK
DAD, LOOK!!
IT'S THE CAHILLS!
AMY, SALADIN TOOK THE MUSIC!!
HE'LL BE FINE! JUST RUN!!!
HMPH.
TRIP
ARGH!!!

AH... EXCUSEZ-MOI, MONSIEUR!
YOU *TRIPPED* ME, YOU CRAZY FOREIGNER!
THAT'S NO FOREIGNER, DAD! IT'S THE CAHILL BRATS' NANNY.
LET GO OF ME OR I'LL SCREAM!
NICE WORK -- KEEP HER ON ICE, HAM! DON'T TAKE YOUR EYES OFF HER FOR A SECOND!

THEY'RE GAINING ON US! KEEP RUNNING!!
BUT WHERE?? THERE'S NOWHERE TO HIDE!
DON'T THEY HAVE SECURITY ON THIS TRAIN? SURELY FRANCE HAS A LAW AGAINST NEANDERTHALS ATTACKING KIDS!
WE CAN'T TALK TO SECURITY! WE CAN'T RISK ANYBODY ASKING QUESTIONS ABOUT WHO WE ARE AND WHAT WE'RE DOING. REMEMBER, SOCIAL SERVICES IS STILL LOOKING FOR US IN BOSTON!
SLAM
KSHHHHHH

AMY! HELP ME BLOCK THE DOOR!
BANG
HEY! IT'S STUCK! GET THIS THING OPEN!!
BANG
BANG
BANG
BANG
BANG
THE NEXT DOOR IS LOCKED!
BANG
BANG
BANG
BANG
BANG

THEY'D NEVER REALLY HURT US, RIGHT?
BANG BANG BANG
BANG BANG BANG
THEY ALMOST TURNED US INTO ROADKILL IN PARIS!
HERE!
YOU CAN'T BE SERIOUS...
CRASH!!
RAHHHH!!!!!

DAN!!
OOP--
CRRACK
GRAB
WHOA...
FWUMP.

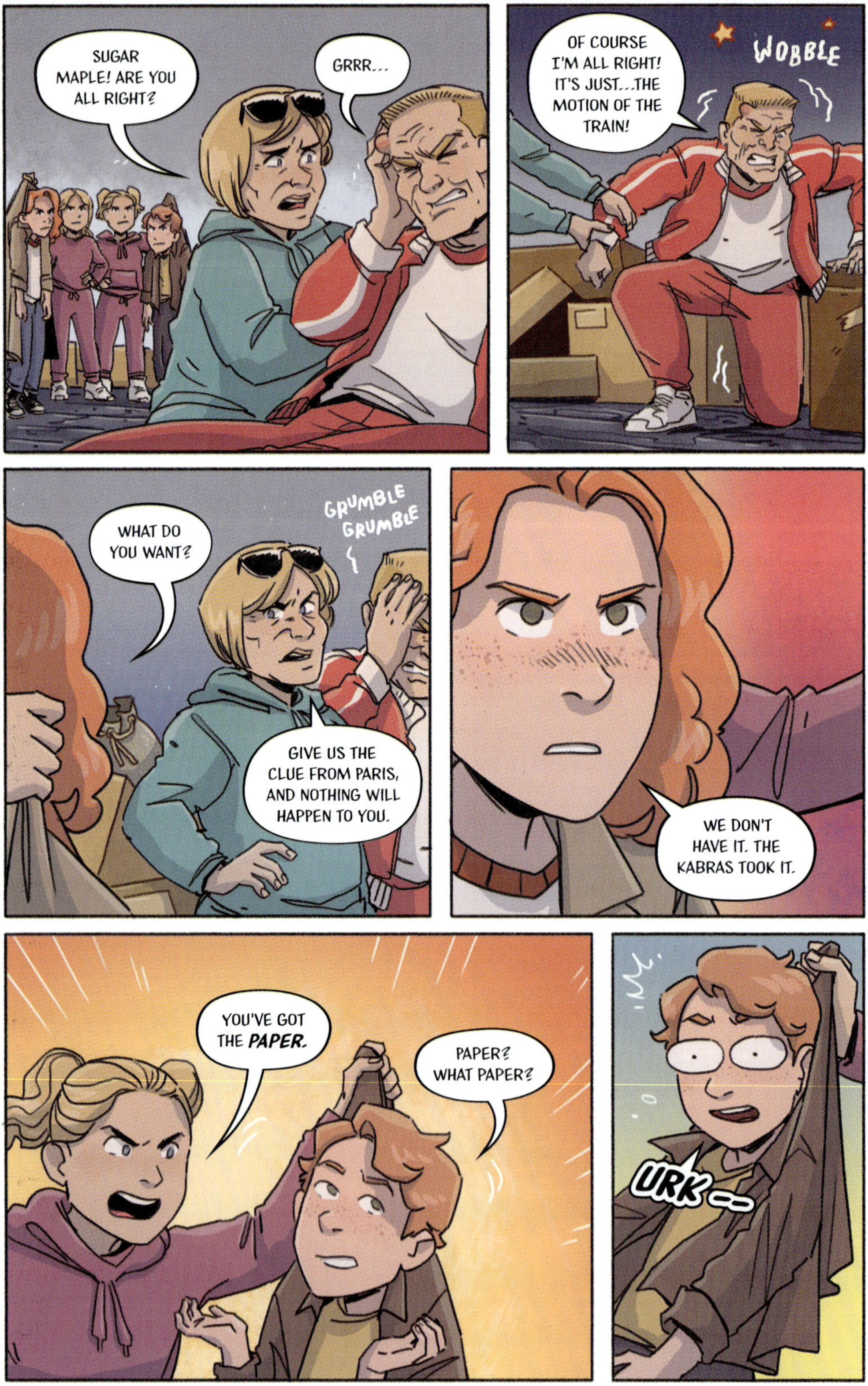
SUGAR MAPLE! ARE YOU ALL RIGHT?
GRRR...
OF COURSE I'M ALL RIGHT! IT'S JUST...THE MOTION OF THE TRAIN!
WOBBLE
WHAT DO YOU WANT?
GRUMBLE GRUMBLE
GIVE US THE CLUE FROM PARIS, AND NOTHING WILL HAPPEN TO YOU.
WE DON'T HAVE IT. THE KABRAS TOOK IT.
YOU'VE GOT THE *PAPER.*
PAPER? WHAT PAPER?
URK--

LISTEN, YOU LITTLE STINK BUG. YOU THINK YOU'RE HOT STUFF BECAUSE YOU TWO WERE GRACE'S FAVORITES...
...BUT TO ME, YOU'RE NOTHING MORE THAN WHAT GETS CLEANED OUT OF THE BOTTOM OF A BIRDCAGE!
COUGH
GASP
SPLUTTER
STOP IT! WE'LL GIVE YOU ANYTHING YOU WANT!
COUGH
HRK
GASP
I TOLD YOU THEY'D FOLD UNDER THE FULL-COURT PRESS.
NOW, MADISON -- AMY DID THE SMART THING. NOT ALL CAHILLS HAVE WHAT IT TAKES.
DAN!!
FWUMP
ARE YOU OKAY??
I'M FINE, I'M FINE...
YOU SHOULDN'T HAVE DONE THAT.
GRACE WOULDN'T WANT US TO GET KILLED. WE'LL FIND ANOTHER WAY.

THAT'S IT... KEEP MARCHING, AND DON'T GET ANY IDEAS.
AMY! DAN! ARE YOU ALL RIGHT?
WE'RE FINE.
SO? WHERE IS IT?
SIGH
...IT'S IN THE OVERHEAD.
NOW, SEE? THAT WASN'T SO HARD, WAS IT --
ARGH!!!
MEOWR

YEOWCH!
MROWR!
OUR CLUE!
YOUR CLUE?!
C'MERE, YOU LITTLE FURBALL! I'M GONNA WRING YOUR NECK --
URP.
WHAT IS GOING ON HERE?
YOU WILL SHOW ME YOUR TICKET FOR THIS TRAIN!
YOU CALL THIS A TRAIN? IF THIS WAS BACK IN THE STATES, I WOULDN'T LET MY GERBIL RIDE THIS RATTLETRAP!
YOU WILL SURRENDER YOUR PASSPORT, MONSIEUR!
AT THE NEXT STATION, YOU WILL TALK TO THE AUTHORITIES!
NO, I DON'T THINK WE WILL.
C'MON, HOLTS --
FAST BREAK!!

WOW. THAT'S SOMETHING YOU DON'T SEE EVERY DAY.
I HATE THEM! NOW WE'VE LOST OUR ONLY LEAD!
IT WASN'T MUCH OF A LEAD, AMY. JUST MUSIC. EVEN IF IT WAS BY MOZART -- BIG WHOOP.
IT *IS* A BIG WHOOP. JUST BECAUSE WE COULDN'T FIND WHAT WAS HIDDEN IN THE PIECE DOESN'T MEAN IT WASN'T THERE.
I WANTED TO AT LEAST PLAY THE NOTES ON A PIANO. MAYBE IT WOULD HAVE TOLD US SOMETHING.
OH! YOU WANT THE NOTES? THAT'S EASY ENOUGH.
YOU CAN'T WRITE MUSIC!
MAYBE NOT... BUT I'VE BEEN STARING AT THAT SHEET SINCE PARIS.

THIS IS IT. I GUARANTEE IT.
DAN, THAT'S AMAZING!
OF COURSE -- YOUR PHOTOGRAPHIC MEMORY! MAYBE YOU AREN'T A TOTAL DOOFUS AFTER ALL...
SALADIN!!!
CHOMP
DON'T EVEN *THINK* ABOUT IT.

ONE TRAIN RIDE LATER...
I SEE THEM.
BAHNHOF CI
THEY ALWAYS LOOK SO... PEDESTRIAN.
AND WHERE'S THEIR LUGGAGE?
A DUFFEL BAG AND BACKPACKS. ARE THEY REALLY THAT POOR?
POOR EXCUSES FOR CAHILLS.
WHAT A STUPID MOVE...I THOUGHT COMPUTERS WERE SUPPOSED TO BE SMART.
IAN, COULD YOU SAVE THE CHESS FOR LATER? SUPERIOR INTELLIGENCE DOESN'T MEAN WE CAN'T STILL MAKE A MESS OF THIS.
WE HAVE THE BOTTLE FROM PARIS -- NONE OF THE OTHER TEAMS STAND A CHANCE. ESPECIALLY NOT THOSE CAHILL CHARITY CASES.
THE CONTEST IS OURS TO WIN.
OR LOSE, IF WE GET OVERCONFIDENT.

BAHNHOFCITY WIEN WEST
WAIT -- THEY'RE GETTING INTO A TAXI.
DRIVER... FOLLOW THAT CAR!

TWO

THE FRANZ JOSEF HOTEL, VIENNA.
I STILL SAY WE SHOULD HAVE STAYED AT THE HOTEL WIENER...
IT'S PRONOUNCED ***VEE-NER...***
AND IT MEANS ANYONE WHO LIVES IN VIENNA -- LIKE BOSTONIANS ARE FROM BOSTON.
IT'S STILL FUNNY. I'M GOING TO GO OVER THERE AND SEE IF I CAN GET ONE OF THEIR SIGNS FOR MY COLLECTION.
WE DON'T HAVE TIME FOR THAT! WE MADE IT TO VIENNA, BUT WE STILL HAVE NO IDEA WHAT TO DO.
WELL, WE CAN STARE AT MUSICAL NOTES UNTIL OUR EYES BUG OUT, BUT IF THE ANSWER'S ANYWHERE... IT'S ***ONLINE.***
YOU THINK YOU CAN GOOGLE THE SOLUTION TO ALL THE WORLD'S PROBLEMS.
NO, BUT I CAN GOOGLE ***MOZART.*** LOOK AT THIS ONE --
THE MOST FAMOUS WIENER OF ALL TIME. I'LL BET THE OSCAR MAYER PEOPLE WOULD HAVE SOMETHING TO SAY ABOUT THAT.

I'M PRETTY SURE IT'S MY JOB TO TELL YOU TO GROW UP.
YOU KNOW, VIENNA IS A REALLY BEAUTIFUL CITY. LOOK AT THE ARCHITECTURE -- I'LL BET SOME OF THOSE BUILDINGS DATE BACK TO THE THIRTEENTH CENTURY!
WOW, IT *IS* BEAUTIFUL!
AND LOOK AT THAT -- I THINK THAT'S THE TOWER OF ST. STEPHEN'S CATHEDRAL.
IT MUST BE AS TALL AS AN OFFICE BUILDING BACK IN THE U.S.!
LOOK, AMY, I REWROTE ALL THAT DUMB MUSIC FOR NOTHING. THE WHOLE THING'S ON THE INTERNET.
WHAT WAS THAT PIECE CALLED AGAIN?
KV 617 -- IT WAS ONE OF THE LAST THINGS MOZART WROTE BEFORE HE DIED.
YEAH, THAT'S IT!
YEAH -- SORT OF. IT'S THE SAME UNTIL HERE, BUT THEN...
IT'S DIFFERENT?
THESE THREE LINES ARE MISSING FROM THE INTERNET VERSION. WEIRD, HUH? IT'S ALMOST LIKE THE WEBSITE LEFT SOMETHING OUT.

OR...MOZART ADDED THREE LINES TO THE MUSIC HE SENT BEN FRANKLIN IN PARIS!
DAN -- WE COULD BE LOOKING AT A SECRET MESSAGE BETWEEN TWO OF THE MOST FAMOUS PEOPLE IN HISTORY!
AND THE EXTRA LINES ARE THE ***CLUE!***
SOUNDS LIKE A LEAD TO ME.
SO... WHERE TO NEXT?

MOZARTHAUS, DOMGASSE 5.
IT'S MOZART, NOT DISNEYLAND! WHAT ARE ALL THESE PEOPLE DOING HERE?
DAN, THIS IS THE ACTUAL APARTMENT MOZART LIVED IN.
THINK ABOUT IT: THE BED WHERE HE SLEPT...THE CHAIR HE SAT IN...THE INKWELL HE USED TO WRITE SOME OF THE GREATEST MUSIC EVER COMPOSED!
SO I'M STANDING IN LINE TO SEE A HOUSE FULL OF OLD FURNITURE?
YES, YOU ARE.
UNTIL WE UNDERSTAND THE MEANING OF THAT CLUE, OUR JOB IS TO LEARN AS MUCH ABOUT MOZART AS WE POSSIBLY CAN.
WHO KNOWS WHEN WE'LL SEE SOMETHING USEFUL?
...IN A CHAIR?
IT'S THE BEST WE'VE GOT.
WE KNOW THE HOLTS ARE ON OUR TRAIL, AND THE REST OF THE COMPETITION CAN'T BE TOO FAR BEHIND THEM.
THEY'RE OLDER THAN US, SMARTER THAN US, AND RICHER THAN US.
WE CAN'T LET UP...NOT EVEN FOR A SECOND.

RULES

EXIT
THANK GOD THAT'S OVER...
AT LEAST BEN FRANKLIN HAD SOME COOL INVENTIONS. THIS GUY JUST SAT AROUND ALL DAY WRITING MUSIC --
DAN! LOOK!
THERE'S A LIBRARY IN THE BASEMENT! A MOZART LIBRARY!
DON'T DO THIS TO ME...
THE ANTIDOTE FOR BORING ISN'T TO FIND SOMETHING EVEN ***BORINGER!***
LIBRARY
HUH...I THOUGHT LIBRARIES WERE SUPPOSED TO HAVE ***BOOKS.***

THE MATERIALS MUST BE OLD AND VALUABLE, SO THEY'RE PROBABLY STORED SOMEWHERE SAFE.
I THINK WE HAVE TO REQUEST WHAT WE WANT ON THE COMPUTER, AND THEN THEY'LL GO GET IT FOR US.
OKAY...LET'S TRY SEARCHING FOR *KV 617.*
AND IF THAT DOESN'T WORK, TRY *BEN FRANKLIN!*
CLICK
HMM...I DON'T SEE ANYTHING IN THE CATALOG. DO YOU?
WHO'S *NANNERL?*
Maria Anna "Na
Mozart
CLICK
WELL, LET'S SEE... MARIA ANNA "NANNERL" MOZART, BORN JULY 30, 1751, IN SALZBURG, AUSTRIA...
DAN! MOZART HAD AN OLDER SISTER!
HE HAS MY SYMPATHY.
NOW I REMEMBER GRACE MENTIONING HER -- SHE WAS JUST AS TALENTED AS MOZART, BUT SHE NEVER GOT THE TRAINING OR THE EXPOSURE BECAUSE SHE WAS A *GIRL.*
AND *LOOK!* HER ORIGINAL DIARY IS RIGHT IN THIS LIBRARY!

I THOUGHT WE WERE LOOKING FOR *MOZART,* NOT HIS SISTER.
IF MOZART WAS A CAHILL, SO WAS NANNERL! MAYBE THERE'S SOMETHING IN HER DIARY WE CAN USE!
EXCUSE ME? WE'D LIKE TO REQUEST THIS BOOK, PLEASE.
THIS IS A HANDWRITTEN DIARY IN THE GERMAN LANGUAGE. DO YOU CHILDREN READ GERMAN?
W-WELL...
WE REALLY NEED TO SEE IT.
ONE MOMENT.
THERE MUST BE *SOMETHING* WE CAN UNDERSTAND -- MAYBE A DRAWING, OR HIDDEN NOTES, LIKE ON FRANKLIN'S STUFF.
GOOD THINKING.

THEY MUST HAVE A PRETTY BIG ARCHIVE DOWN HERE TO FIT ALL THAT STUFF WE SAW ON THE COMPUTER...
I WONDER IF IT'S HARD TO KEEP TRACK OF IT ALL --
EEK!
HALLO? HALLO?!
POLIZEI! POLIZEI!
THAT MEANS POLICE!
DO YOU THINK SHE SOMEHOW FOUND OUT WE'RE WANTED BY SOCIAL SERVICES BACK IN MASSACHUSETTS?
HOW COULD SHE? WE DIDN'T EVEN TELL HER OUR NAMES!
CHILDREN? WHERE ARE YOU?!
AH, I AM SO SORRY! THIS IS A TERRIBLE TRAGEDY!
THE DIARY -- IT'S MISSING!
NANNERL'S DIARY HAS BEEN STOLEN!

THREE

BACK AT THE FRANZ JOSEF HOTEL...
STILL WON'T TOUCH YOUR FOOD, HUH?
C'MON, SALADIN...I KNOW YOU'RE USED TO THE GOOD LIFE, BUT THAT'S OVER NOW. THERE'S NO RED SNAPPER WHERE ***WE'RE*** GOING.
YOU AND I ARE THE ***ADULTS*** HERE... WE'RE SUPPOSED TO HAVE THINGS FIGURED OUT.
MROW...
KER-CLICK
SPEAKING OF AMY AND DAN...
SIGHHHHHH
UH-OH... ROUGH MORNING?

OH, IT WAS A BLAST.
PICTURE A MILLION-YEAR-OLD HOUSE FULL OF DUSTY FURNITURE AND AN ESSAY TO READ ON EVERY WALL, AND WHEN YOU FINALLY FIND SOMETHING YOU ACTUALLY WANT TO LOOK AT... IT'S NOT EVEN THERE.
FLOP
WE REQUESTED A BOOK IN THE MUSEUM LIBRARY, BUT WHEN THEY WENT TO GET IT FOR US, IT WAS MISSING.
THE LIBRARIAN SAID THAT'S NEVER HAPPENED BEFORE... THEY CALLED THE POLICE AND EVERYTHING!
KZZT
CLICK
-- AT THE ROYAL HABSBURG HOTEL YESTERDAY, WHERE FANS GATHERED IN DROVES...
JUST OUR ROTTEN LUCK, I GUESS...
HEY, ISN'T THAT --
TO SEE THEIR FAVORITE INTERNATIONAL STAR, STREAMER AND INFLUENCER...
JONAH WIZARD!!!
HE'S HERE IN VIENNA?!
BUT WHY??

HE MUST BE ON A PROMOTIONAL TOUR FOR HIS NEW SINGLE...
I WAS JUST READING ABOUT IT -- APPARENTLY THE SONG DROPS TOMORROW.
THAT'S JUST A COVER! HE'S HERE BECAUSE HE KNOWS THE NEXT CLUE IS ABOUT ***MOZART!***
OR HE'S WORKING WITH THE HOLTS...THEY MUST HAVE CHECKED WHERE OUR TRAIN WAS HEADED.
HOLD ON A SEC...
DAN, LOOK! THAT'S WHERE WE WERE TODAY -- DOMGASSE!
YOU'RE RIGHT! THERE'S THE MOZARTHAUS A COUPLE OF DOORS DOWN.
AND LOOK -- IT'S THAT OLD LIBRARIAN, THE ONE WHO CALLED OUT THE SWAT TEAM OVER A MISSING DIARY!
WOW... NOT REALLY MY IDEA OF A TYPICAL ***WIZARD*** FAN.
WAIT --
WHAT IF IT'S NO ACCIDENT JONAH PICKED THAT SPOT FOR HIS PRESS CONFERENCE?
WHAT IF HE DID IT THERE TO CREATE A DISTRACTION SO HE COULD STEAL NANNERL'S DIARY FROM THE MOZARTHAUS?

THAT WOULD MAKE SENSE...EXCEPT THERE HE IS ON-SCREEN, WITH TWENTY CAMERAS ON HIM, STEALING NOTHING.
WHEN HAVE WE EVER SEEN JONAH WITHOUT HIS FATHER STANDING RIGHT BEHIND HIM?
JONAH HELD THE CONFERENCE TO GIVE HIS DAD THE CHANCE TO SNEAK INTO THE MOZARTHAUS AND SWIPE THE DIARY!
AMY, YOU WERE RIGHT -- THE DIARY ***IS*** IMPORTANT!
YEAH... AND NOW THE ENEMY HAS IT.
WELL, THEY STOLE IT FROM THE MUSEUM... WHY CAN'T WE STEAL IT FROM ***THEM?***
WHOA, WHOA, WHOA, HANG ON --
THERE'S A BIG DIFFERENCE BETWEEN SEARCHING FOR CLUES AND ***ROBBING*** PEOPLE.
AS LONG AS I'M YOUR BABYSITTER --
AU PAIR.
-- I'M NOT GOING TO STAND BY AND LET YOU TWO SWITCH OVER TO THE DARK SIDE!
BUT THEN WE'LL ***LOSE!***

AS MUCH AS I HATE TO AGREE WITH DAN, HE'S GOT A POINT.
I KNOW STEALING IS WRONG, BUT THIS CONTEST IS TOO HUGE FOR US TO WORRY ABOUT BEING THE GOOD GUYS.
AMY...
NELLIE, WE BARELY KNEW OUR PARENTS BEFORE THEY DIED. GRACE WAS ALL WE HAD, AND NOW SHE'S GONE, TOO.
THE CONTEST IS A BIG DEAL FOR EVERYBODY, BUT FOR US...IT'S ALL WE HAVE.
WE CAN'T DO THIS HALFWAY. WE HAVE TO GO ALL OUT. AND THAT MEANS LOOKING FOR CLUES WHEREVER THEY ARE -- EVEN INSIDE SOMEBODY ELSE'S HOTEL ROOM.
I UNDERSTAND IF YOU DON'T WANT TO BE INVOLVED, BUT WE'RE GOING TO DO THIS...WITH OR WITHOUT YOU.
MRRP.
HMM. YOU THINK YOU CAN GET RID OF ME THAT EASILY?
FAT CHANCE. THIS MAY BE YOUR SHOW, BUT I STILL MAKE THE RULES.
BUCKLE UP, KIDS...WE'VE GOT A HEIST TO PLAN!

THE ROYAL HABSBURG HOTEL.
OKAY, SO THE LAUNCH PARTY FOR JONAH'S NEW SINGLE IS AT EIGHT...

HE'LL PROBABLY TALK WITH REPORTERS FOR A FEW MINUTES, AND THEN HEAD OVER TO EUROTAINMENT TV, WHICH IS HOSTING THE BASH. THE WIZARDVERSE FAN PAGE SAYS THAT EVERYBODY WHO'S ANYBODY IS GOING TO BE THERE.
I THOUGHT YOU QUIT BEING A JONAH WIZARD FAN WHEN YOU MET HIM IN PARIS.
I'M HELPING YOU ROB THE GUY, AREN'T I?
QUICK! GET DOWN!
THERE HE IS!
THANK YOU, THANK YOU...
THANKS FOR COMIN' OUT...
YOU'RE TOO KIND!
JONAH, CAN WE EXPECT ANY EXCLUSIVES FOR YOUR EUROPEAN FANS?
ANY TRUTH TO THE RUMOR THAT YOU'RE DATING?
HAVE YOU HEARD THAT THE SUPER GRIP ON YOUR ACTION FIGURE FLUNKED SAFETY INSPECTION?
C'MON...LET'S SNEAK IN THE SIDE DOOR WHILE THEY'RE DISTRACTED.

NUR FÜR
TORISIERTE
TARBEITER
WE'LL NEED TO STAY OUT OF SIGHT...THAT SAYS *"EMPLOYEES ONLY."*
YOU SPEAK GERMAN?
IT'S MORE LIKE A WORKING KNOWLEDGE...
WUMMMMMMMMM
SO WHERE IS EVERYBODY? IT'S LIKE A GHOST TOWN DOWN HERE...
I GUESS MOST OF THE STAFF MUST WORK THE DAY SHIFT.
JACKPOT!

JUST GIVE ME A MINUTE TO CHANGE.
DON'T YOU THINK YOUR **HAIR** MIGHT GIVE YOU AWAY?
AH, THE STUFFED SHIRTS IN THIS PLACE COULD USE A LITTLE LIVENING UP.
OKAY, COME ON. EVERYBODY IN THE CART.
HOW ARE WE GONNA KNOW WHAT ROOM HE'S IN?
THE ROYAL SUITE, OF COURSE! WOULD ANYTHING LESS BE GOOD ENOUGH FOR THE GREAT **JONAH WIZARD**?
AND KEEP IT DOWN! LAUNDRY DOESN'T TALK.
SQUEAKA SQUEAKA SQUEAKA

WOW... SO THIS IS LIFESTYLES OF THE RICH AND FAMOUS...
1700
OKAY, YOU TWO CAN COME OUT N--
DOES A MAID NOT KNOCK AT HIS HIGHNESS'S DOOR?
1700
UH -- I'M SORRY, I THOUGHT THE SUITE WAS EMPTY. I'M SUPPOSED TO BRING FRESH TOWELS TO THE WIZARDS' ROOM.
STUFF
STUFF
MY DEAR YOUNG LADY, THIS IS THE SUITE OF HIS HIGHNESS THE GRAND DUKE OF LUXEMBOURG. THE AMERICAN TELEVISION ACTOR IS IN THE SUITE BELOW --
AND A GREAT FUSS HE MADE ABOUT THAT, I MIGHT ADD.
SORRY, SIR. I'LL GET OUT OF YOUR WAY.
SQUEAKA
SQUEAKA
SQUEAKA
A MOMENT, IF YOU PLEASE.
NOW THAT YOU ARE HERE, HIS HIGHNESS'S BEDCHAMBER REQUIRES REFRESHING.

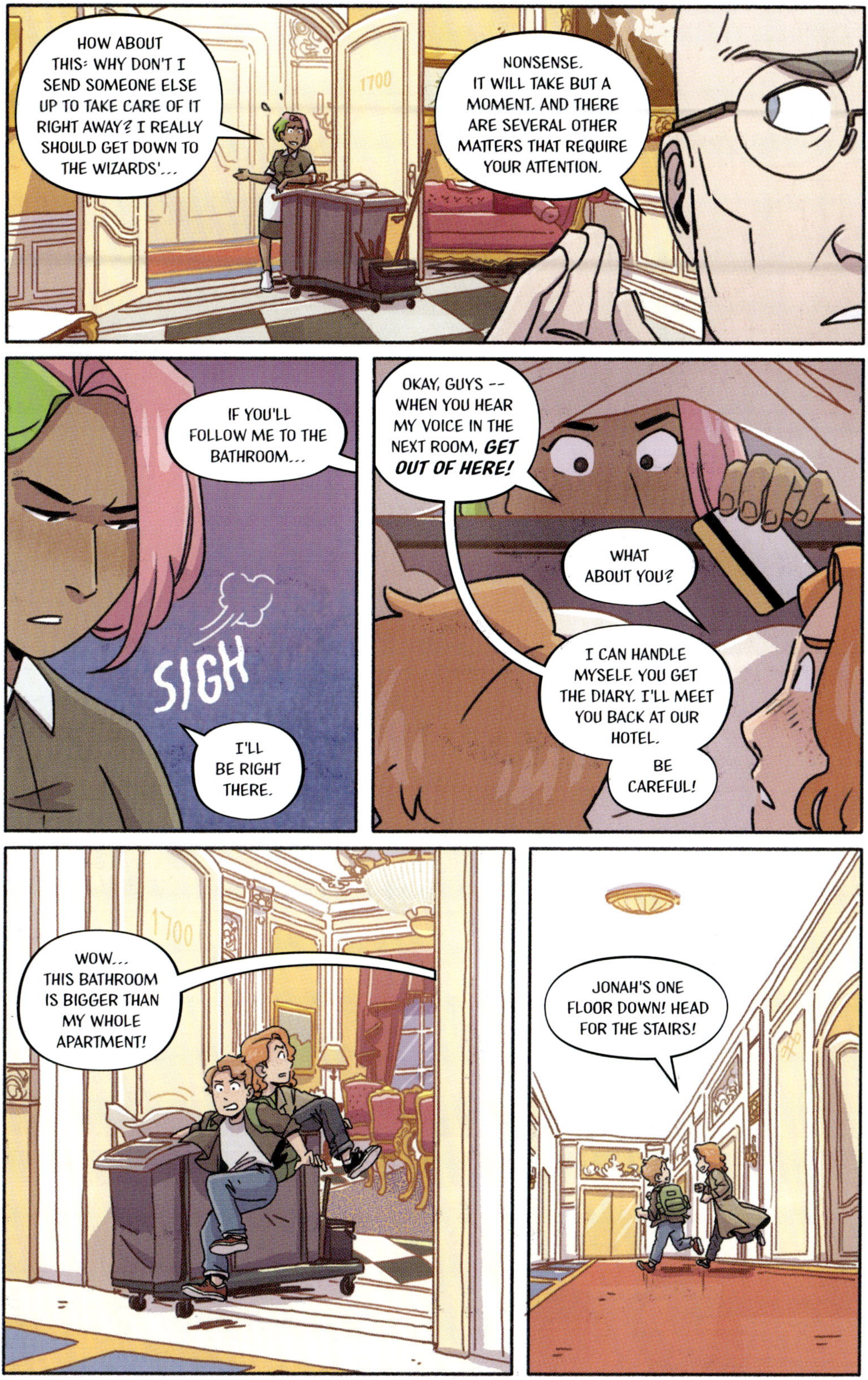
HOW ABOUT THIS: WHY DON'T I SEND SOMEONE ELSE UP TO TAKE CARE OF IT RIGHT AWAY? I REALLY SHOULD GET DOWN TO THE WIZARDS'...
1700
NONSENSE. IT WILL TAKE BUT A MOMENT. AND THERE ARE SEVERAL OTHER MATTERS THAT REQUIRE YOUR ATTENTION.
IF YOU'LL FOLLOW ME TO THE BATHROOM...
SIGH
I'LL BE RIGHT THERE.
OKAY, GUYS -- WHEN YOU HEAR MY VOICE IN THE NEXT ROOM, ***GET OUT OF HERE!***
WHAT ABOUT YOU?
I CAN HANDLE MYSELF. YOU GET THE DIARY. I'LL MEET YOU BACK AT OUR HOTEL.
BE CAREFUL!
1700
WOW... THIS BATHROOM IS BIGGER THAN MY WHOLE APARTMENT!
JONAH'S ONE FLOOR DOWN! HEAD FOR THE STAIRS!

1600 -- THIS MUST BE IT.
BEEP
OKAY...NOW, IF I WERE MR. WIZARD, WHERE WOULD I HIDE THE DIARY I STOLE?
ZIP

HEY, AMY, CHECK IT OUT...
IT'S JONAH WIZARD, LIVE FROM VIENNA! DON'T FORGET TO SMASH THAT LIKE!
FIGURES
PUT THAT BACK! IT'S BAD ENOUGH WE BROKE INTO HIS ROOM. WE DON'T NEED TO STEAL HIS DUMB TOYS.
IT'S FOR MY ***COLLECTION!*** HE'S GOT A WHOLE BOX OF THEM ANYWAY.
SNAP
GR6
CLICK
WHOA -- NO WONDER THE ***SUPER GRIP*** IS BEING RECALLED! YOU COULD CRACK A WALNUT WITH THIS THING!
WAIT! DO THAT AGAIN -- I SAW SOMETHING!
SURE, JUST GIMME YOUR FINGER...
NO, DAN, LOOK! IT'S SOME KIND OF SECRET CODE!
GR63K
CLICK
YEAH, IT'S A ***CODE --***
TO DOWNLOAD A FREE JONAH WIZARD REMIX FROM HIS WEBSITE!
DO YOU LIVE UNDER A ROCK? I'VE SEEN A MILLION ADS ABOUT IT ONLINE.
OH. WELL, I GUESS THE ALGORITHM MUST KNOW I'M TOO ***MATURE*** FOR THAT SORT OF THING...

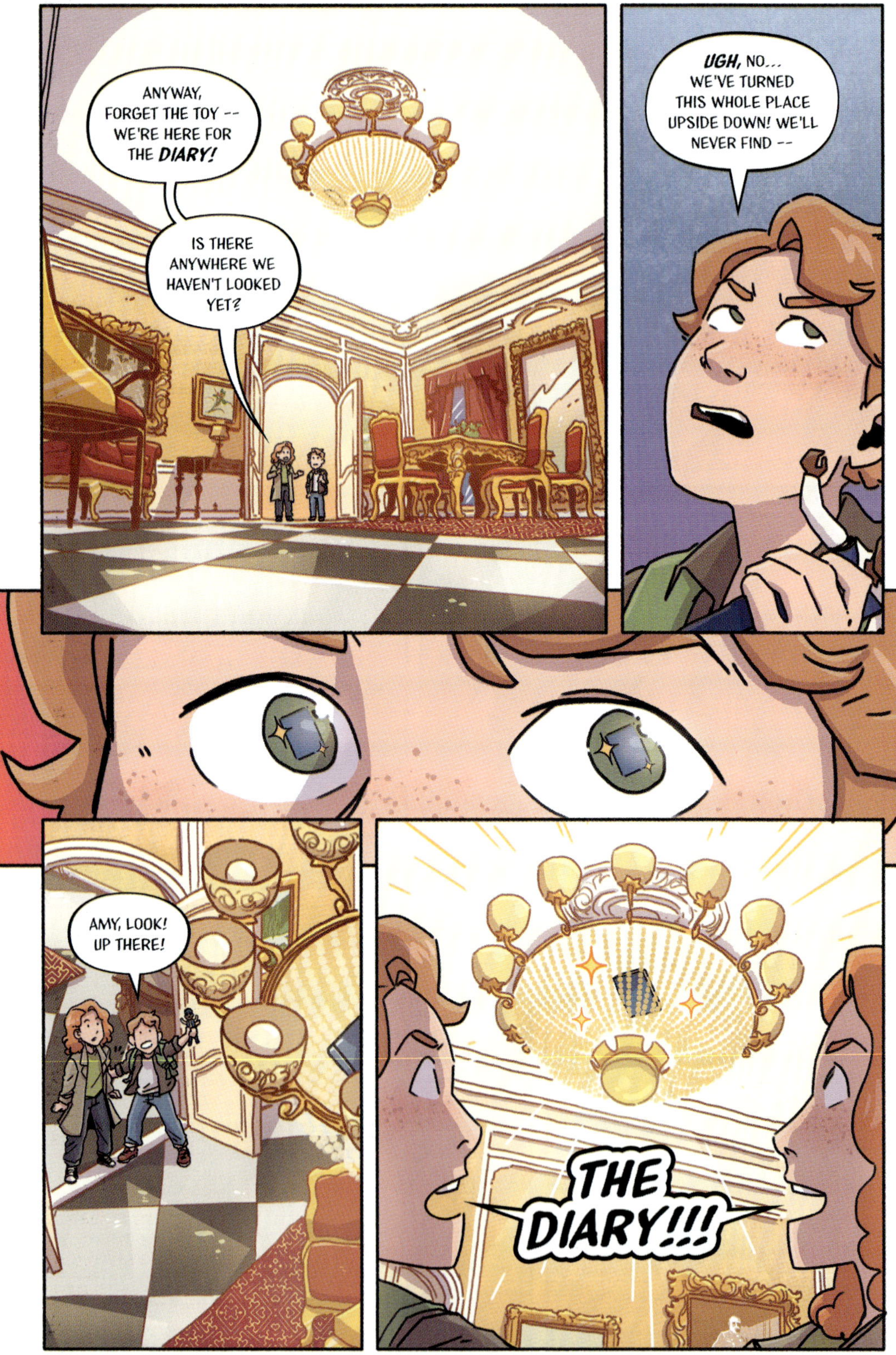
ANYWAY, FORGET THE TOY -- WE'RE HERE FOR THE *DIARY!*
IS THERE ANYWHERE WE HAVEN'T LOOKED YET?
UGH, NO... WE'VE TURNED THIS WHOLE PLACE UPSIDE DOWN! WE'LL NEVER FIND --
AMY, LOOK! UP THERE!
THE DIARY!!!

DAN, COME HELP ME WITH THE TABLE.
SCRAAPE
OKAY, HAND ME A CHAIR.
GUH...
ALMOST THERE...
JUST A LITTLE CLOSER...
GOT IT!!

MEANWHILE, UPSTAIRS...
SCRUB SCRUB
I CAN'T BELIEVE I'M DOING THIS...THOSE KIDS OWE ME *BIG*.
IF WE ALL MAKE IT OUT OF HERE IN ONE PIECE, THAT IS...
AHEM.
YOU DO NOT WORK FOR US, FRÄULEIN. WHAT ARE YOU DOING IN THIS SUITE?
WHAT? OF COURSE I WORK HERE.
DO YOU THINK I SNEAK INTO HOTELS TO SCRUB TOILETS FOR *FUN*?
YOU DO NOT WORK HERE.
OH, SO YOU KNOW EVERY SINGLE EMPLOYEE?
NO...BUT YOUR HAIR COLOR -- IT IS AGAINST HOTEL POLICY.
YOU WILL COME WITH ME.

...
ALL RIGHT, YOU CAUGHT ME.
BUT I'M HERE BY *MISTAKE!* I WAS TRYING TO GET INTO *JONAH WIZARD'S* SUITE --
I'M HIS BIGGEST FAN. I JUST WANTED TO MEET HIM... BUT I PICKED THE WRONG ROOM.
AND YOU ARE DOING THIS CRIME ALONE? NO ONE IS WITH YOU?
YES, OF COURSE! I'M TOTALLY ALONE... AND IT'S NOT A *CRIME* TO LOVE JONAH WIZARD. HE'S JUST THE COOLEST --
CRASH
CRASH
TINKLE
CLANG
SMASH
FRÄULEIN, YOU HAD BETTER HOPE THAT THIS DISTURBANCE HAS NOTHING TO DO WITH YOU, OR YOU WILL BE ENJOYING A GREAT DEAL MORE OF OUR AUSTRIAN HOSPITALITY... IN *PRISON*.

OH NO...
OOF...WHAT HAPPENED?
IT DOESN'T MATTER. WE'VE GOT TO GET OUT OF HERE -- HALF THE HOTEL MUST HAVE HEARD THAT CRASH!
AMY! RUN!!!
WAIT! YOU CAN'T LEAVE! WHAT IF JONAH IS LYING IN THERE, BLEEDING?
STUPID GIRL! YOUR HERO IS NOT EVEN IN THE BUILDING!
<SEND A GUARD TO THE BOTTOM OF EVERY ELEVATOR AND STAIRWELL IMMEDIATELY!>
<NO ONE LEAVES THIS HOTEL UNTIL I SAY SO!>

DING
HUMMMMMMMMM
THEY COULD BE WAITING FOR US IN THE LOBBY.
BUT THAT'S WHERE THE EXIT IS! YOU CAN'T LEAVE FROM THE SECOND FLOOR!
SURE, YOU CAN.
HOW?!
BY JUMPING.
HAVE YOU LOST YOUR --

NO WAY, DAN! I'M NOT JUMPING! WE'LL BREAK OUR LEGS!
IT'S OKAY! LOOK DOWN!
ROYAL HABSBURG HOTEL

PIECE OF CAKE...
A SHORTER DROP THAN THE HIGH DIVING BOARD.
BUT NO WATER!
DAN!

BOING
G HOTEL
SEE? NO PROBLEM!
HURRY UP!

I CAN'T DO IT...
I CAN'T...
IT'S ONE THING TO HUNT CLUES, BUT *JUMPING OFF OF BUILDINGS??*
MAYBE I'M NOT BRAVE ENOUGH TO BE A CAHILL AFTER ALL.
I'M GOOD AT LOTS OF OTHER THINGS...BUT NOT *THIS.*
I'M SORRY, GRACE.
"WE CAN'T DO THIS HALFWAY.
"WE HAVE TO GO ALL OUT."

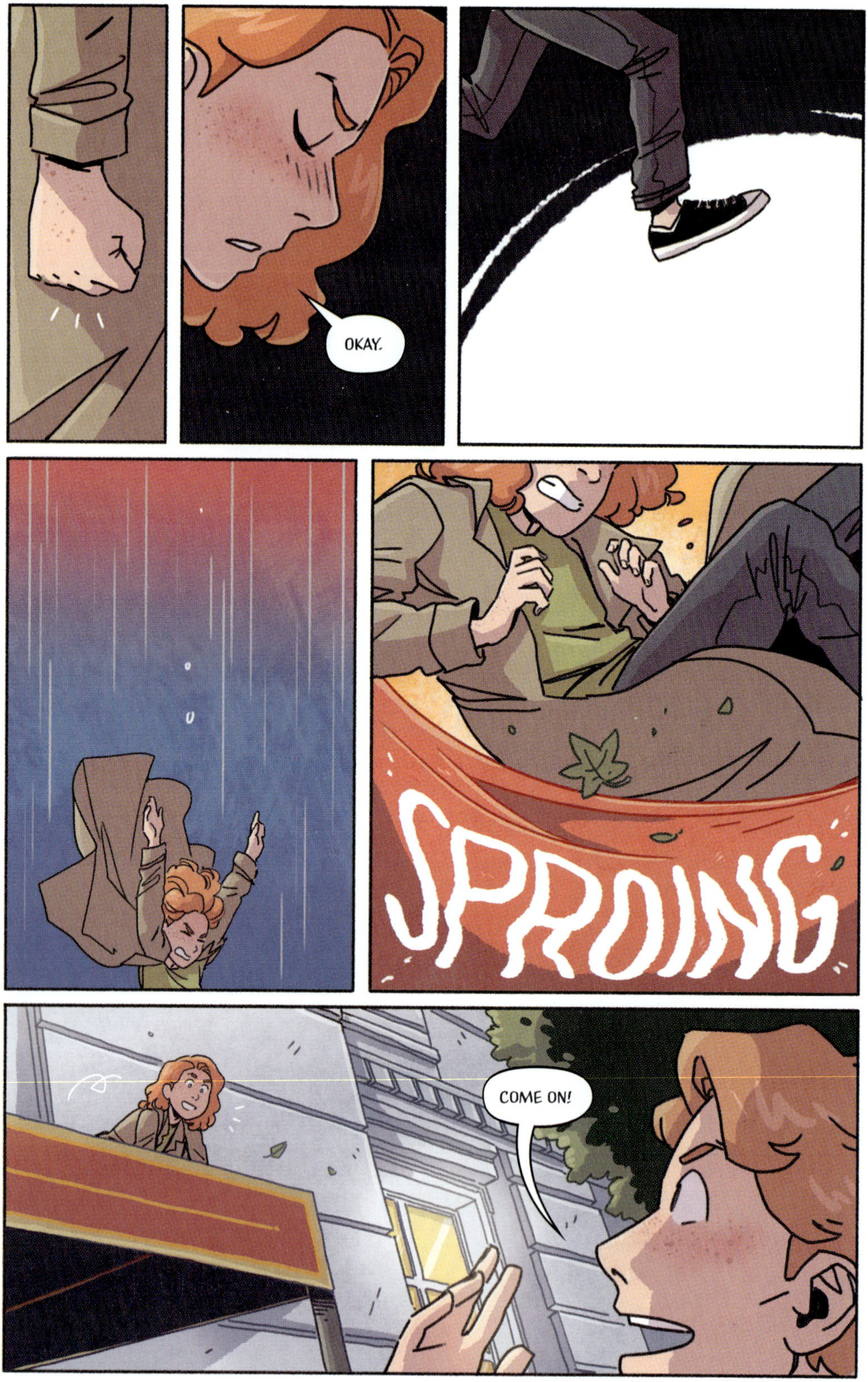
OKAY.
SPROING
COME ON!

NELLIE --
I KNOW...

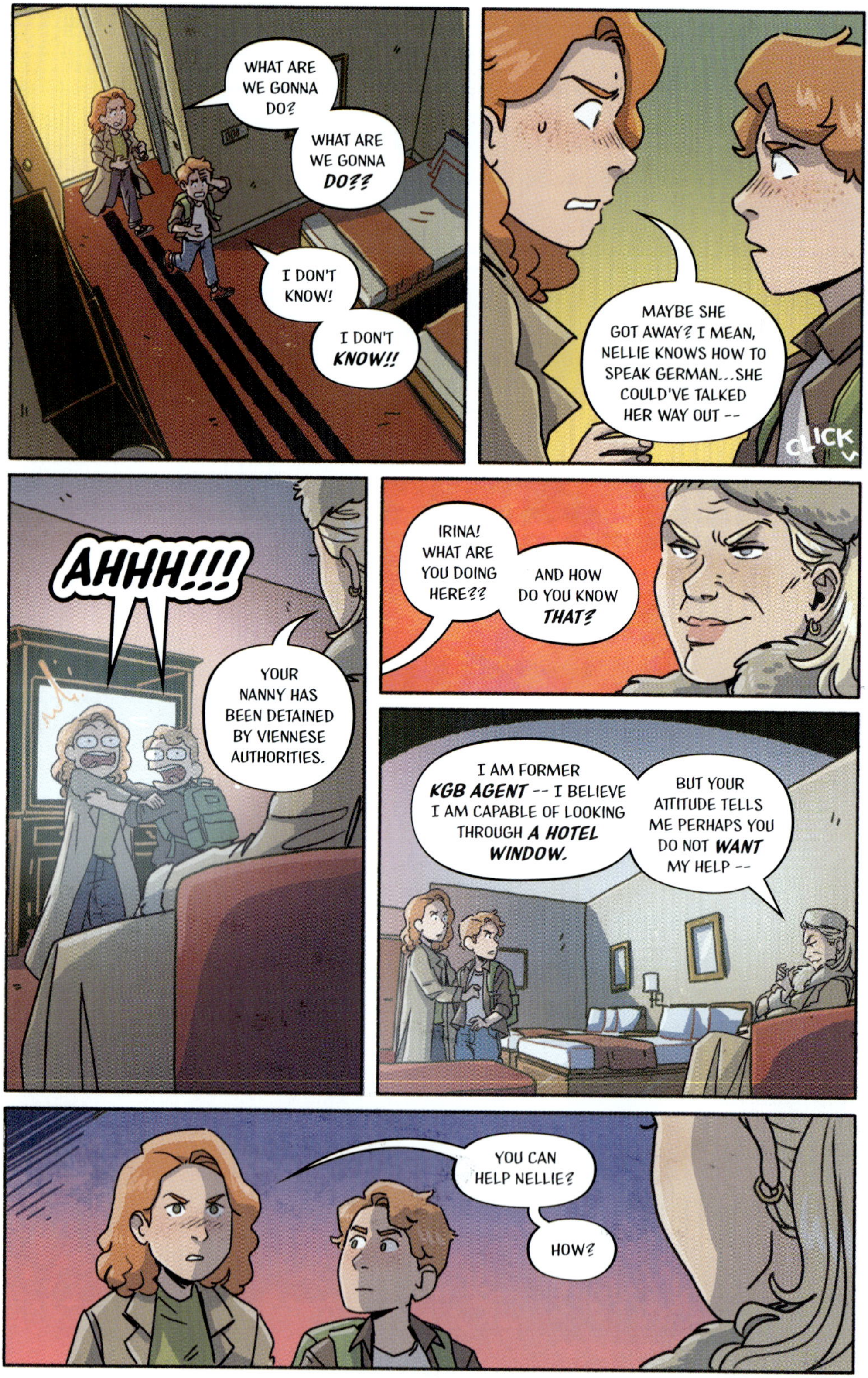
WHAT ARE WE GONNA DO?
WHAT ARE WE GONNA **DO??**
I DON'T KNOW!
I DON'T **KNOW!!**
MAYBE SHE GOT AWAY? I MEAN, NELLIE KNOWS HOW TO SPEAK GERMAN...SHE COULD'VE TALKED HER WAY OUT --
CLICK
AHHH!!!
YOUR NANNY HAS BEEN DETAINED BY VIENNESE AUTHORITIES.
IRINA! WHAT ARE YOU DOING HERE??
AND HOW DO YOU KNOW **THAT?**
I AM FORMER **KGB AGENT** -- I BELIEVE I AM CAPABLE OF LOOKING THROUGH **A HOTEL WINDOW.**
BUT YOUR ATTITUDE TELLS ME PERHAPS YOU DO NOT **WANT** MY HELP --
YOU CAN HELP NELLIE?
HOW?

WHAT IS IT YOUR BUSINESS, SO LONG AS SHE IS RETURNED TO YOU? I JUST REQUIRE ONE SIMPLE THING...
THE ITEM YOU REMOVED FROM THE HOTEL ROOM OF OUR OBNOXIOUS COUSIN JONAH WIZARD.
NO DEAL!
A WORD OF ADVICE...YOU SHOULD NOT LET THIS IMPETUOUS LITTLE BOY SPEAK FOR YOU.
PERHAPS YOU SHOULD NOT LET HIM SPEAK AT ALL.
IN KGB, WE FOUND DUCT TAPE TO BE BOTH EFFECTIVE AND AFFORDABLE.
OKAY, FINE...
YOU CAN HAVE THE --
ITEM WE TOOK.
ZIP

HERE.
A CHILD'S PLAYTHING? YOU ARE NOT SERIOUS.
YOU ASKED FOR WHAT WE TOOK. THIS IS IT.
IT ONLY SEEMS LIKE AN ACTION FIGURE.
CHECK THIS OUT.
CLICK
SNAP
SEE? IT'S --
GR63K
A CODE?!

THERE IS NO NEED FOR SMALL TALK IN A BUSINESS TRANSACTION. WE HAD A SIMILAR DEVICE IN THE KGB. CRUDE, BUT EFFECTIVE.
EXPECT YOUR NANNY SHORTLY.
SLAM
DAN!!!
I CAN'T BELIEVE YOU DID THAT!
WHAT IF IRINA KNEW ABOUT THE DIARY?
SHE DIDN'T!
BUT SHE ***COULD*** HAVE! WHAT IF SHE HAD SEEN THE ADS ABOUT THE REMIX?!
RIGHT, CUZ ***SHE'S*** THE TARGET AUDIENCE...
YOU RIPPED OFF A RUSSIAN SPY! YOU COULD HAVE GOTTEN NELLIE KILLED, AND MAYBE US, TOO!
WHY ARE YOU YELLING AT ME ABOUT WHAT ***DIDN'T*** HAPPEN? WE SHOULD BE CELEBRATING!
WHO'S CELEBRATING...?

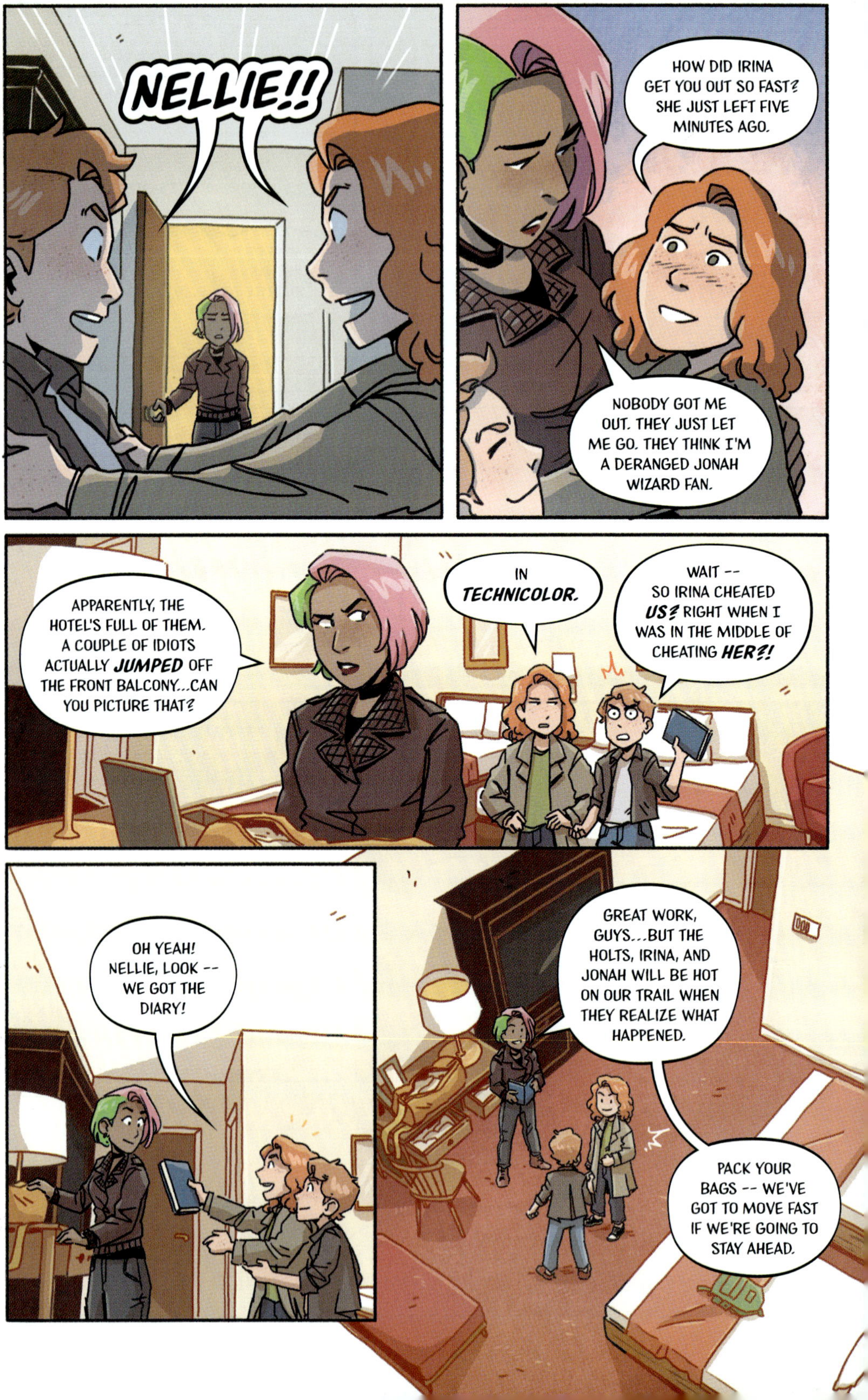
NELLIE!!
HOW DID IRINA GET YOU OUT SO FAST? SHE JUST LEFT FIVE MINUTES AGO.
NOBODY GOT ME OUT. THEY JUST LET ME GO. THEY THINK I'M A DERANGED JONAH WIZARD FAN.
APPARENTLY, THE HOTEL'S FULL OF THEM. A COUPLE OF IDIOTS ACTUALLY JUMPED OFF THE FRONT BALCONY...CAN YOU PICTURE THAT?
IN TECHNICOLOR.
WAIT -- SO IRINA CHEATED US? RIGHT WHEN I WAS IN THE MIDDLE OF CHEATING HER?!
OH YEAH! NELLIE, LOOK -- WE GOT THE DIARY!
GREAT WORK, GUYS...BUT THE HOLTS, IRINA, AND JONAH WILL BE HOT ON OUR TRAIL WHEN THEY REALIZE WHAT HAPPENED.
PACK YOUR BAGS -- WE'VE GOT TO MOVE FAST IF WE'RE GOING TO STAY AHEAD.

BACK IN SUITE 1600...
YOU PROMISED JONAH EXTRA SECURITY!
WE BELIEVE IT WAS HARMLESS, MEIN HERR. A LOVESICK GIRL.
YOUR TALENTED SON HAS THIS EFFECT ON HIS FANS, YES?
EXCUSE ME...
HOW WOULD YOU DESCRIBE THIS SUPERFAN WHO LOVES ME SO MUCH SHE BROKE INTO MY ROOM?
OH...YOUNG LADY, EARLY TWENTIES...
WITH QUITE AN UNUSUAL HAIRSTYLE -- HALF GREEN, HALF PINK.
WOULD YOU GIVE US A MOMENT? I NEED TO HAVE A PRIVATE WORD WITH MY SON.
SOUNDS LIKE THE CAHILL KIDS' NANNY... WHICH MEANS THEY MUST BE HERE IN VIENNA.
THEY CAN'T HAVE GOTTEN FAR. PERHAPS WE CAN USE YOUR MOTHER'S EUROPEAN CONTACTS TO --
NO... NO NEED.
WE'RE STILL ONE STEP AHEAD -- WE KNOW SOMETHING ABOUT THE DIARY THEY DON'T...
YET.

FOUR

FIND ANYTHING GOOD?
WUMMMMMMMMMMM
IT'S A TRAGEDY... NANNERL WAS ONE OF THE GREATEST MUSICIANS OF HER TIME -- EVERY BIT AS BRILLIANT AS HER BROTHER.
AND YET VERY FEW PEOPLE HAVE EVEN HEARD OF HER... SHE WASN'T TAKEN AS SERIOUSLY JUST BECAUSE SHE WAS A GIRL.
I MEAN... I NEVER HEARD OF HER **BROTHER,** EITHER -- NOT UNTIL THIS CONTEST.
YOU'D STILL RECOGNIZE A LOT OF HIS MUSIC, THOUGH. WHAT ABOUT, "TWINKLE, TWINKLE, LITTLE STAR"?
EXACTLY. WE CAN ONLY GUESS WHAT NANNERL MIGHT HAVE CONTRIBUTED IF SHE'D BEEN ALLOWED TO DEVELOP HER TALENTS.
YEAH, BUT DID SHE CONTRIBUTE ANY ***CLUES?***
THERE ARE NO NOTES SCRIBBLED IN THE MARGINS OR ANYTHING LIKE THAT...
WELL, YOU'LL HAVE PLENTY OF TIME TO KEEP LOOKING IN THE CAR --
HOLD IT!

THERE ARE PAGES MISSING HERE! AT LEAST TWO. LOOK!
WHY WOULD HE BOTHER TO HIDE THE DIARY IN THE CHANDELIER IF HE'D ALREADY TAKEN THE IMPORTANT PARTS OUT OF IT?
WHOA... DO YOU THINK JONAH DID IT?
TO THROW US OFF THE TRAIL OF THE REAL STUFF?
MAYBE... BUT THOSE PAGES COULD HAVE BEEN REMOVED ANYTIME IN THE LAST 200 YEARS.
FOR ALL WE KNOW, NANNERL CUT THEM OUT HERSELF BECAUSE SHE SPILLED INK ON THEM!
DING
NO OFFENSE, YOU GUYS, BUT I'VE BEEN AROUND YOUR FAMILY LONG ENOUGH TO KNOW THIS HAS CAHILL WRITTEN ALL OVER IT. I'VE NEVER SEEN SUCH A BUNCH OF BACKSTABBERS IN MY LIFE.
LOBBY
SHE'S RIGHT... EVERY TIME WE THINK WE'RE MAKING PROGRESS, SOMEONE TURNS OUT TO BE A STEP AHEAD OF US.
BUT THE REAL CLUE ISN'T THE DIARY -- IT'S THE ***MUSIC.*** AND WE'RE THE ONLY ONES WHO HAVE THAT!
WHICH GIVES ME AN IDEA -- LET'S TRY ***ONE LAST THING*** BEFORE WE LEAVE.

PLAY THE NEW STUFF... THE PART THAT ISN'T IN THE REAL SONG.
MAYBE A TRAPDOOR WILL OPEN, OR WE'LL CALL UP THE CAHILL GENIE OR SOMETHING.
OKAY, UM... IT STARTS LIKE THIS...
CLAP
CLAP
WAIT, YOU ALL KNOW THIS SONG? IS IT BY MOZART?
CLAP
CLAP
CLAP
NEIN -- NOT MOZART.
IT IS AN OLD CLASSIC, AN AUSTRIAN FOLK SONG CALLED "DER ORT, WO ICH GEBOREN WAR," WHICH IN YOUR LANGUAGE MEANS...

"THE PLACE WHERE I WAS BORN."
SO THE SONG WAS A SECRET MESSAGE BETWEEN MOZART AND BEN FRANKLIN!
EXACTLY. MOZART MUST HAVE BEEN ASKING HIM TO COME TO THE TOWN WHERE HE WAS BORN...

SALZBURG, AUSTRIA!

IT'S BEAUTIFUL!
BUT BIGGER THAN I EXPECTED.
NELLIE, WE HAVE NO IDEA WHAT WE'RE LOOKING FOR, OR EVEN WHERE TO START.
SEEMS PRETTY STRAIGHTFORWARD. THE SONG IS "THE PLACE WHERE I WAS BORN."
WE'LL GET A GUIDEBOOK AND FIND THE ACTUAL HOUSE WHERE MOZART GREW UP.
OH, NO YOU DON'T. YOU'RE NOT DRAGGING ME TO ANOTHER MOZART HOUSE. NOT WHEN I HAVEN'T RECOVERED FROM THE LAST ONE --
LOOK OUT!!
SKREEEEEE
UGH, CAN YOU BELIEVE THIS JAYWALKING MORON --
WAIT! DON'T HONK! GET DOWN!
LOOK WHO IT IS...

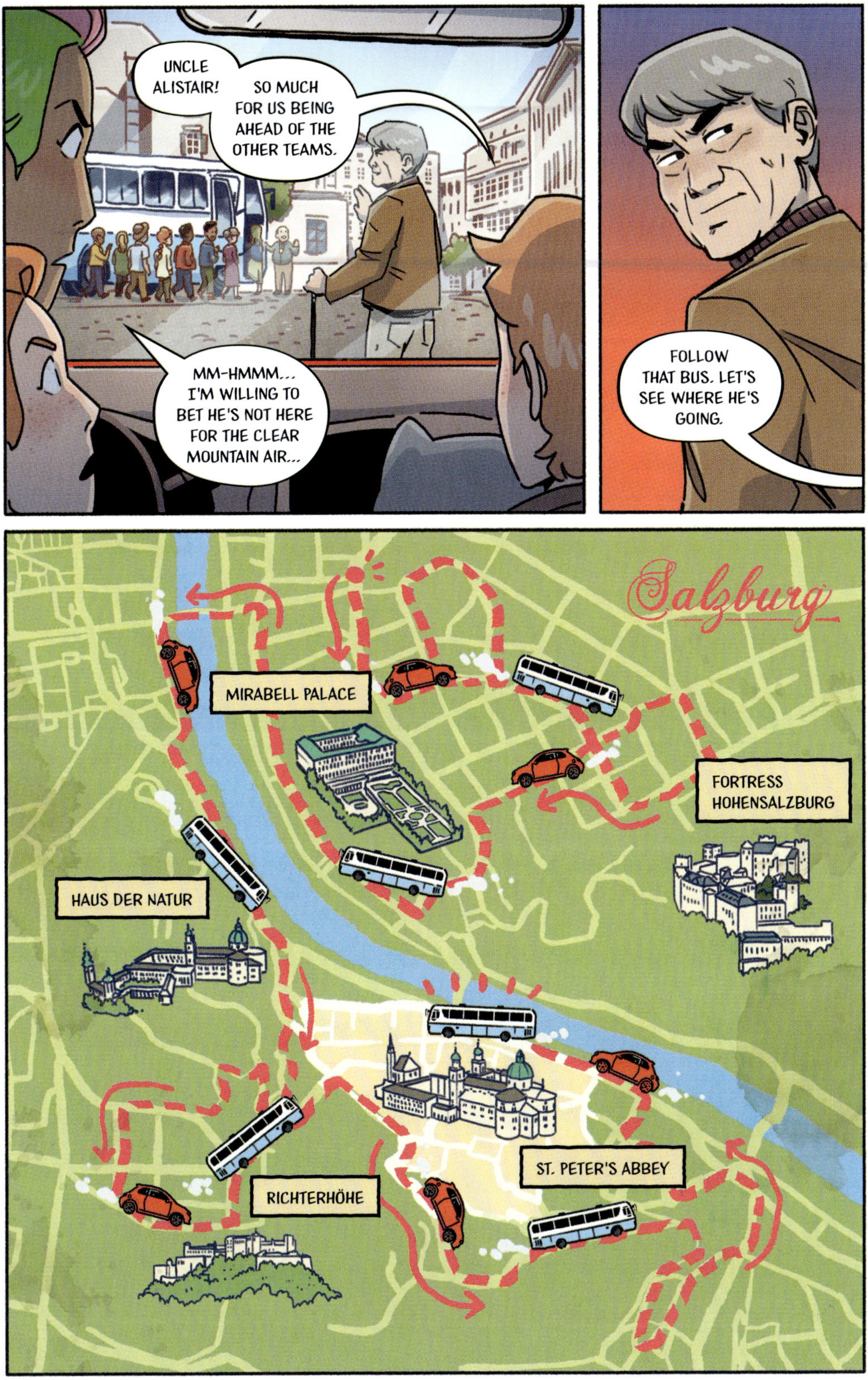
UNCLE ALISTAIR!
SO MUCH FOR US BEING AHEAD OF THE OTHER TEAMS.
MM-HMMM... I'M WILLING TO BET HE'S NOT HERE FOR THE CLEAR MOUNTAIN AIR...
FOLLOW THAT BUS. LET'S SEE WHERE HE'S GOING.
Salzburg
MIRABELL PALACE
FORTRESS HOHENSALZBURG
HAUS DER NATUR
ST. PETER'S ABBEY
RICHTERHÖHE

SAINT PETER'S ABBEY...
SO, YOU THINK YOUR NEXT CLUE COULD BE IN THERE?
ALISTAIR CERTAINLY SEEMS TO THINK SO.
St. Peter's Abbey
NELLIE, WHY DON'T YOU FIND A HOTEL AND TRY AGAIN TO GET SALADIN TO EAT?
WE'LL BE LESS CONSPICUOUS IF WE SPLIT UP.
MROWR...
ALL RIGHT. I'LL BE BACK HERE IN AN HOUR. DON'T GET YOURSELVES KILLED.
WHOA... THERE'S A *CEMETERY* HERE, TOO? COOL...
St. Peter's
THIS SAYS THE ABBEY IS MORE THAN THIRTEEN HUNDRED YEARS OLD...
AND THE OLDEST GRAVES IN THE CEMETERY DATE BACK TO THE TWELFTH CENTURY!
THAT MEANS SOME OF THESE PEOPLE HAVE BEEN DEAD FOR ALMOST A *THOUSAND* YEARS...
NEAT.
DAN, LOOK AT THIS!

IT ALSO SAYS THE REMAINS OF NANNERL MOZART ARE HERE!
WE'RE GOING TO DIG UP A DEAD BODY? AWESOME!
SHHH! OF COURSE NOT!
BUT WHAT IF MOZART PLANTED A CLUE ON HIS SISTER?
MOZART DIED BEFORE NANNERL.
NOW, WE'RE LOOKING FOR A COMMUNAL TOMB. THAT'S WHERE THE BROCHURE SAYS SHE'S BURIED.
OH, LIKE A CONDO FOR DEAD PEOPLE?
SHOW SOME RESPECT -- ONE OF THE OTHERS IN HER CRYPT IS MICHAEL HAYDN, THE FAMOUS COMPOSER!
OH YEAH? WHAT'S HE DOING NOW...
...DECOMPOSING?
DON'T BE GROSS. COME ON.

YOU'RE NOT FORGOTTEN, NANNERL. PEOPLE ARE STARTING TO APPRECIATE YOU AS A GENIUS IN YOUR OWN RIGHT.
WHAT'S THE BIG FASCINATION WITH ***NANNERL*** MOZART? SO SHE WAS AS GOOD AS HER BROTHER. SO WHAT?
DON'T YOU SEE HOW UNFAIR THAT IS? SHE NEVER GOT THE CREDIT JUST BECAUSE SHE WAS A ***GIRL.***
I AGREE, SHE GOT A RAW DEAL. BUT NOW THAT SHE'S BEEN IN THIS CRYPT FOR A COUPLE HUNDRED YEARS, WHAT DIFFERENCE DOES IT MAKE TO HER?
IT MAKES A DIFFERENCE TO ***ME.***
HOW DO YOU THINK I'D FEEL IF YOU WERE CONSIDERED THIS WHIZ KID PRODIGY AND I WAS NOBODY, WHEN WE WERE EQUALLY GOOD AT THE SAME THING?
THAT COULD NEVER HAPPEN TO US. WE'RE NOT GOOD AT ***ANY*** OF THE SAME THINGS.
HEY, WHAT'S THAT?

WHO PUTS A HOUSE HALFWAY UP A CLIFF?
THAT MUST BE THE ENTRANCE TO THE SALZBURG CATACOMBS.
CATACOMBS? AGAIN?
WELL, NOT THE PAVED-WITH-BONES KIND...BUT IT SAYS THERE ARE TUNNELS IN THAT HILL.
IF THERE'S A CLUE AT ST. PETER'S, I'LL BET THAT'S WHERE IT IS.
AND THE COMPETITION JUST PULLED AHEAD OF US.
COME ON!

...THERE ARE MULTIPLE GUESTS IN THE CATACOMBS TODAY, SO AS WE PASS OTHER GROUPS, PLEASE STAY TO THE RIGHT...
COUGH
WHEW... IT'S MUSTY DOWN HERE...
DID YOU BRING YOUR INHALER?
YEAH, I HAVE IT. AS LONG AS WE --
COUGH
-- DON'T KICK UP TOO MUCH DUST, IT SHOULD BE FINE.
COMING THROUGH, COMING THROUGH...
TO THE RIGHT, EVERYONE, TO THE ***RIGHT...***

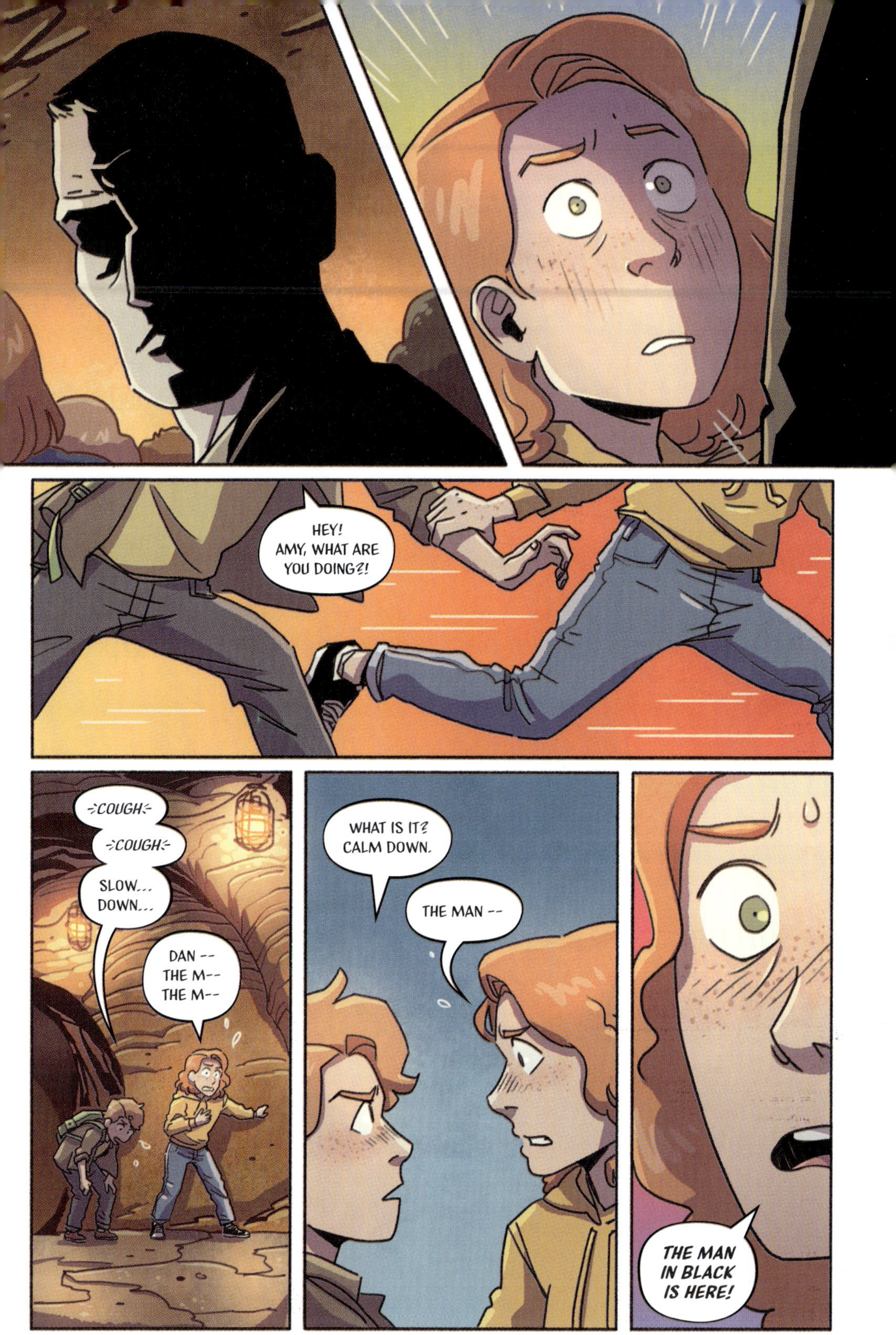
HEY! AMY, WHAT ARE YOU DOING?!
-COUGH-
-COUGH-
SLOW... DOWN...
DAN -- THE M-- THE M--
WHAT IS IT? CALM DOWN.
THE MAN --
THE MAN IN BLACK IS HERE!

DID HE SEE YOU?
I'M NOT SURE... BUT HE ALWAYS SHOWS UP WHEN SOMETHING TERRIBLE IS ABOUT TO HAPPEN -- FIRST THE FIRE AT GRACE'S MANSION, THEN THE BOMB AT THE FRANKLIN INSTITUTE!
WE'VE GOT TO GET OUT OF HERE!
NOT UNTIL WE FIND WHAT WE CAME FOR. UNCLE ALISTAIR **AND** THE MAN IN BLACK?
THAT'S DOUBLE PROOF WE'RE ON THE RIGHT TRACK!
O-OKAY. YOU'RE RIGHT.
LET'S KEEP GOING.
SEE ANY MARKINGS? OR STRANGE SYMBOLS?
NOTHING YET...
I KEEP THINKING I SEE CARVINGS IN THE STONES, BUT THEY'RE JUST OLD, BUMPY ROCKS --
BYOOoooo.

DAN! DAN!!
THE LIGHTS! WHERE ARE YOU?!
IT'S OKAY, I'M RIGHT --
AHHH!!! WHAT JUST TOUCHED ME?!
CALM DOWN, AMY, IT'S ME! THIS IS PROBABLY JUST A POWER FAILURE!
AND THE MAN IN BLACK JUST *HAPPENS* TO BE HERE?
IF WE CAN'T SEE HIM, HE CAN'T SEE US, RIGHT?
WHO KNOWS? MAYBE HE'S JUST AS LOST AS WE ARE.
OR MAYBE HE'S BACK THERE SOMEWHERE, WAITING FOR US!
WE'LL HAVE TO CHANCE IT. ALL WE CAN DO IS RETRACE OUR STEPS AND HOPE FOR THE BEST.
HERE... GIMME YOUR HAND.
SEE, YOU RUN *YOUR* HAND ALONG ONE WALL OF THE PASSAGE, AND I'LL RUN *MY* HAND ALONG THE OTHER.
WE WON'T MISS ANY TURNS THAT WAY.
DAN, I DON'T THINK I CAN DO THIS. I'M TOO SCARED.
IT'S OKAY, AMY...IT'S THE SAME TUNNEL.
WE MADE IT HERE -- WE CAN MAKE IT BACK.

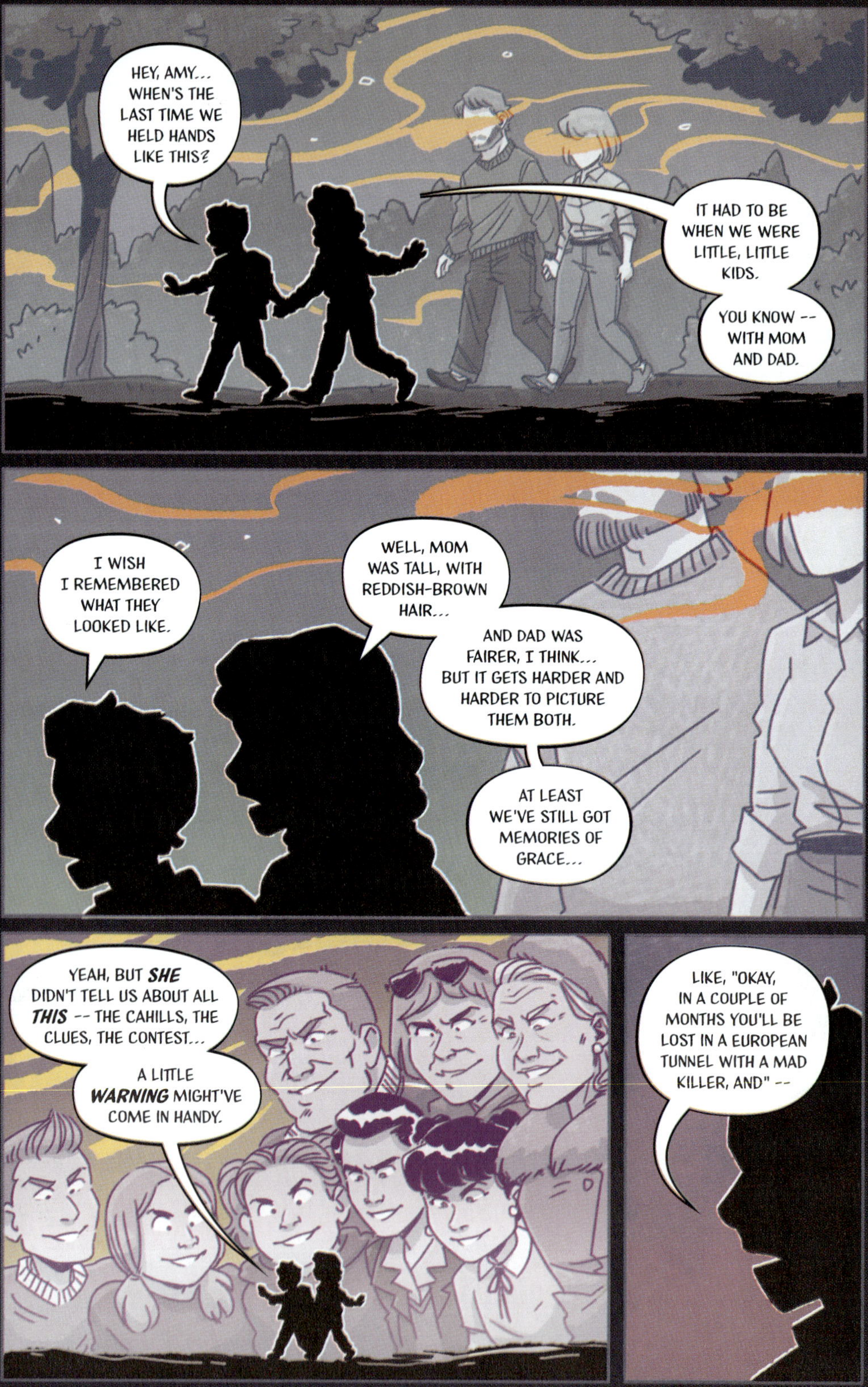
HEY, AMY... WHEN'S THE LAST TIME WE HELD HANDS LIKE THIS?
IT HAD TO BE WHEN WE WERE LITTLE, LITTLE KIDS.
YOU KNOW -- WITH MOM AND DAD.
I WISH I REMEMBERED WHAT THEY LOOKED LIKE.
WELL, MOM WAS TALL, WITH REDDISH-BROWN HAIR...
AND DAD WAS FAIRER, I THINK... BUT IT GETS HARDER AND HARDER TO PICTURE THEM BOTH.
AT LEAST WE'VE STILL GOT MEMORIES OF GRACE...
YEAH, BUT SHE DIDN'T TELL US ABOUT ALL THIS -- THE CAHILLS, THE CLUES, THE CONTEST...
A LITTLE WARNING MIGHT'VE COME IN HANDY.
LIKE, "OKAY, IN A COUPLE OF MONTHS YOU'LL BE LOST IN A EUROPEAN TUNNEL WITH A MAD KILLER, AND" --

BOOM
AH! AMY!
DAN!

ARE YOU HURT?
-COUGH- -COUGH-
I'M OKAY... BUT I THINK THE WAY BACK IS BLOCKED NOW.
OH GOD... A CAVE-IN? AND NOW WE'RE TRAPPED DOWN HERE IN THE DARK? I DON'T WANNA DIE IN THE DARK. I CAN'T EVEN SEE --
KSST
WAIT -- DAN, WAS THAT YOUR INHALER? I CAN SEE YOU!
YEAH, I SEE YOU, TOO! JUST YOUR OUTLINE. BUT --
THAT MEANS THERE HAS TO BE LIGHT COMING FROM SOMEWHERE.
AND WHERE THERE'S LIGHT, THERE'S --
A WAY OUT!
THERE... THROUGH THAT ARCHWAY!
A SECRET PASSAGE!
HOLD ON... I'LL CHECK IT OUT FIRST.
WHOA -- AMY, GET DOWN HERE!

LOOK AT ALL THESE BARRELS! COULD THEY BE A CLUE?
HMM... WELL, THEY WON'T DO US MUCH GOOD IF WE DON'T KNOW WHAT'S INSIDE THEM.
MAYBE WE CAN --
UNGH!
-- SWIPE ONE AND ROLL IT OUT OF HERE.
WOBBLE WOBBLE
GUH!!--
A LITTLE HELP HERE?
FORGET THE BARREL, DAN -- LOOK AT THIS!
IT'S A FORMULA...
FOR WHAT?
OUR VERY FIRST CLUE WAS AN INGREDIENT -- IRON SOLUTE, REMEMBER?
MAYBE THIS IS THE WHOLE RECIPE.
WE'VE GOT TO TAKE THIS BACK TO NELLIE. SHE'LL BE ABLE TO TELL US WHAT IT SAYS.

WE'RE ALREADY LATE. DO YOU THINK NELLIE WILL COME LOOKING FOR US IF WE DON'T SHOW UP?
IF THAT'S HER PLAN, I HOPE SHE'S GOT ONE OF THOSE GIANT MINING DRILLS...
SUNLIGHT!
I DON'T BELIEVE IT! WE DID IT!
DAN, WE REALLY DID IT! WE MADE IT OUT IN ONE P--

MEANWHILE, OUTSIDE...
THEY'RE HALF AN HOUR LATE, SALADIN. WHERE CAN THEY BE?
St. Peter's Abbey
I MEAN, I KNOW THEY'RE JUST KIDS, BUT WHEN I WAS THEIR AGE, I KNEW THE MEANING OF PUNCTUALITY...
IF I HAD EVER DISAPPEARED ON MY PARENTS FOR HOURS AT A TIME, I'D HAVE GOTTEN AN EARFUL!
BUT MAYBE KIDS THESE DAYS ARE USED TO BEEING MORE INDEPENDENT? WHO KNOWS...
I JUST WISH THEY WOULD COMMUNICATE --
GO, GO, GO!!!
DRIVE! DRIVE!!

SKREEEEEEE
WHAT WAS THAT? WHAT HAPPENED BACK THERE?!
IT'S NOT OUR FAULT! THOSE GUYS ARE CRAZY! THEY'RE LIKE MINI DARTH VADERS WITHOUT THE MASK!
THEY'RE BENEDICTINE MONKS! THEY'RE MEN OF PEACE! MOST OF THEM ARE UNDER VOWS OF SILENCE!
YEAH, WELL, NOT ANYMORE... THEY CURSED US OUT PRETTY GOOD.
I DON'T KNOW THE LANGUAGE, BUT SOME THINGS YOU DON'T HAVE TO TRANSLATE.
NELLIE, WE FOUND A CLUE, AND THEY DIDN'T WANT US TO TAKE IT. I'M POSITIVE IT'S SOMETHING IMPORTANT!
CAN YOU TELL US WHAT IT SAYS?
WHY DON'T WE PUT SOME DISTANCE BETWEEN OURSELVES AND THE ABBEY FIRST.
HOW'D YOU LIKE TO HAVE TO EXPLAIN TO THE RENTAL COMPANY THAT THEIR CAR WAS TRASHED BY AN ARMY OF RAGING MONKS?

A FEW MINUTES LATER...
...OKAY.
LET'S HAVE A LOOK AT THIS "CLUE."
WE THINK IT MIGHT BE SOME KIND OF FORMULA!
OH...
OH MY GOD...
I DON'T BELIEVE IT...
THAT GOOD, HUH?
BUT WHAT'S THE FORMULA *FOR?*
ARE... YOU...

...KIDDING ME?!
THIS ISN'T A CLUE --
IT'S THE RECIPE FOR BENEDICTINE!
BENEDICTINE? YOU MEAN THE DRINK?
IT'S AN ANCIENT RECIPE KNOWN ONLY TO THE BENEDICTINE BROTHERS FOR CENTURIES. THAT'S WHY THEY WERE CHASING YOU!
OHHH...
WE ALMOST GOT KILLED IN THERE... AND IT WAS ALL FOR NOTHING.
NO WONDER THE MONKS WERE UPSET. IT MUST HAVE SEEMED LIKE WE STOLE THE MOST IMPORTANT THING THEY OWN.
WELL, MAYBE IT ISN'T A CLUE, BUT AT LEAST THAT PARCHMENT WILL LOOK COOL IN MY COLLECTION.
DAN! WE HAVE TO GIVE THAT BACK!
GOOD LUCK. IF WE SET FOOT IN THAT ABBEY AGAIN, THOSE MEN OF PEACE WILL RIP OUR HEADS OFF.

WE'RE REALLY SORRY, NELLIE. WE'LL FIND A WAY TO MAIL IT BACK TO THEM, WE JUST THOUGHT --
HEY, WAIT A MINUTE -- WHERE'S SALADIN'S COLLAR?
OH, I WAS GOING TO TELL YOU -- BEFORE I HAD TO PLAY GETAWAY DRIVER FROM THE **CHRISTIAN BROTHERS...**
I TOOK SALADIN TO A VETERINARY CLINIC, BECAUSE HE **STILL** WOULDN'T EAT --
HE'S FINE BY THE WAY, JUST BEING PICKY --
BUT DURING THE EXAM, **THIS** FELL OUT OF HIS COLLAR.
WHAT IS IT?
DON'T YOU EVER WATCH TV? IT'S A HOMING DEVICE. YOU PLANT IT ON SOMEBODY WHEN YOU WANT TO KEEP TRACK OF WHERE THEY'RE GOING.
YEAH, BUT WHO KEEPS TRACK OF A **CAT?**

NOT THE CAT -- US! OUR COMPETITION DID THIS!
THAT'S WHY WE CAN'T GET AHEAD IN THE CONTEST -- WHEREVER WE GO, SOMEONE ELSE ALWAYS KNOWS ABOUT IT.
THIS HAS THE KABRAS WRITTEN ALL OVER IT!
LEAVE IT TO A COUPLE OF RICH KIDS TO BUY A HIGH-TECH WAY TO CHEAT BECAUSE THEY'RE TOO DUMB TO GET THE CLUES ON THEIR OWN.
OR IRINA. THIS WOULD BE KID STUFF FOR THE KGB.
IT COULD BE ANY OF THEM -- EVEN MR. MCINTYRE! REMEMBER -- HE WAS TAKING CARE OF SALADIN AT THE MANSION AFTER GRACE DIED.
SO WHAT DO WE DO WITH THE TRANSMITTER NOW? SMASH IT?
OR DROP IT DOWN THE SEWER! LET THE CHEATERS GO SCUBA DIVING FOR IT.
YOU KNOW, THIS COULD BE A GOLDEN OPPORTUNITY TO PUT THE COMPETITION OFF OUR SCENT. WE SHOULDN'T WASTE IT ON A JOKE.
AW, YOU'RE NO FUN...
TRUST ME, THIS WILL BE FUN... LOOK WHO JUST SHOWED UP!
NOW LISTEN, HERE'S THE PLAN...

AH...I'M GETTING TOO OLD FOR ALL THIS RUNNING AROUND.
IT'S A GOOD THING THE PRIZE IS WORTH IT.
I HOPE THOSE KIDS ARE OKAY, THOUGH...THAT EXPLOSION IN THE CATACOMBS WAS BIGGER THAN I EXPECTED.
BUT I SUPPOSE THAT'S THE COST OF PLAYING THE GAME. AMY AND DAN WILL HAVE TO GROW UP SOONER OR LATER.
UNSCREW
THEY NEED TO LEARN THAT LIFE ISN'T ALL RAINBOWS AND BUTTERFLIES... YOU HAVE TO HAVE YOUR WITS ABOUT YOU!
?
PULL
AFTER ALL, WE ARE ALL ADVERSARIES... **SOMEONE** HAS TO LOSE.

I SHOULD KNOW -- YOU DON'T BUILD UP A LEGENDARY MICROWAVE BURRITO EMPIRE WITHOUT KNOCKING A FEW HEADS TOGETHER...
BUT THEN AGAIN, MAYBE I'M BEING TOO HARSH.
I SHOULD CHECK ON THE KIDS. THEY ARE GRACE'S GRANDCHILDREN...
DROP
I'LL CHECK THE NEWS WHEN I GET BACK TO MY HOTEL, JUST TO MAKE SURE THEY GOT OUT OKAY.
BUT THAT'S IT. CAN'T BE GOING SOFT, NOW -- THAT'S HOW YOU LOSE...
...AND I AM NOT A LOSER.
REPLACE
ON WITH THE HUNT!

FIVE

THE NEXT DAY.
WOLFGANG AMADEUS MOZART 1770 VENEZIA
THIS PAPER YOU FOUND IN UNCLE ALISTAIR'S CANE... IT ISN'T GERMAN.
NO? I JUST ASSUMED, BECAUSE WE'RE IN AUSTRIA -- UH, WHAT IS IT, THEN?
ITALIAN, I THINK. NOT ONE OF MY LANGUAGES.
SO HOW DO YOU KNOW IT'S ITALIAN, THEN?
VERY FUNNY, WISE GUY... SPANISH AND ITALIAN AREN'T TOO DIFFERENT.
AND THERE'S A WORD AT THE TOP -- VENEZIA. I'M PRETTY SURE THAT'S VENICE, WHICH IS IN ITALY.
IT ALSO SAYS 1770 -- HE PERFORMED ALL ACROSS ITALY AROUND THEN. HIS FATHER TOOK HIM ON TOUR.
SO THIS IS... AN EIGHTEENTH-CENTURY CONCERT POSTER, STARRING MOZART?
IN VENICE. THAT'S WHERE THE NEXT CLUE MUST BE HIDDEN.
I ALWAYS WANTED TO GO TO VENICE. IT'S SUPPOSED TO BE THE ROMANCE CAPITAL OF THE WORLD.
TOO BAD YOUR DATE IS A CAT ON A HUNGER STRIKE.
HA HA... BETTER THAN AN ELEVEN-YEAR-OLD WITH A BIG MOUTH.

A FEW HOURS LATER...
ARE YOU **STILL** LOOKING AT THAT PAPER? WHAT ARE YOU TRYING TO DO? LEARN ITALIAN BY ***OSMOSIS?***
THERE'S A NAME ON HERE I CAN'T FIGURE OUT. WHO'S ***FIDELIO RACCO?***
ANOTHER MUSICIAN?
I DON'T THINK SO... MOZART AND HIS SISTER WERE A PACKAGE DEAL. I NEVER READ ANYTHING ABOUT A THIRD PERFORMER ON THEIR TOURS.
WELL, IF IT REALLY IS A CONCERT POSTER, MAYBE THIS RACCO GUY IS LIKE... A ***PROMOTER.***
HEY... THAT'S NOT A BAD IDEA.
I MEAN...NOT A PROMOTER LIKE THEY HAVE TODAY. BUT BACK THEN, VISITING MUSICIANS GAVE PRIVATE SHOWS AT RICH PEOPLE'S MANSIONS.
MAYBE FIDELIO RACCO HOSTED MOZART AND NANNERL.
VENEZIA
I WONDER IF WE CAN FIND OUT WHERE HE LIVED...

MAN...WE'VE BEEN IN TRAFFIC FOR HOURS...I GUESS VENICE IS THE ***PLACE TO BE*** TODAY...
WHOA! GET DOWN!
HUH? WHY?
WHAT'S GOING ON? ARE WE IN DANGER?!
SHHHH...LOOK WHO'S IN FRONT OF US...
W1Z4RD
THE LICENSE PLATE...IS THAT WHO I THINK IT IS?!
W1Z4RD
NELLIE, WE ***GOTTA*** FOLLOW THAT LIMO!
OKAY, I'LL STAY A FEW CARS BACK. LET'S SEE WHAT OUR OLD PAL JONAH IS UP TO...

DON'T GET TOO CLOSE...
BUT DON'T LOSE HIM!
WILL YOU TWO JUST LET ME DRIVE??
GREAT... I THOUGHT WE WERE GOING TO VENICE, BUT THAT SIGN SAYS TRONCHETTO.
SMOOTH MOVE, AMY -- NOW WE'RE DRIVING TO THE WRONG TOWN.
TRONCHETTO
NO, WE'RE NOT...LOOK!

VENICE... JUST LIKE IN PICTURES.

PRETTY COOL...
TOO BAD THAT'S NOT WHERE THIS ROAD LEADS, THOUGH. IT LOOKS LIKE WE'RE HEADED DOWN TO THAT OTHER ISLAND.
IT LOOKS LIKE A PARKING LOT?
MORE LIKE THE ***GREAT-GRANDDADDY*** OF THEM.
SEE, THERE ARE NO CARS ALLOWED IN VENICE! YOU HAVE TO PARK AT TRONCHETTO AND TAKE A FERRY TO THE CITY.
THEN HOW DO PEOPLE GET AROUND OVER THERE?
BY BOAT. VENICE IS CRISSCROSSED BY DOZENS OF CANALS.

HUH... I WONDER HOW JONAH KNEW TO COME HERE...
I HAVE NO IDEA...
AND NOW HE'S STANDING IN LINE WITH THE COMMON PEASANTS? HOW DO YOU FIGURE THAT?
I'M STARTING TO DIG THIS "NO CARS" THING. IT'S A GREAT EQUALIZER.
JONAH CAN AFFORD TO BUY THAT FERRY AND KICK EVERYBODY ELSE OFF. IF HE'S TAKING A PUBLIC BOAT, IT'S BECAUSE HE'S TRYING TO SLIP INTO TOWN UNNOTICED.
LET'S PARK THE CAR AND SEE WHERE HE'S GOING.
COME ON! IF WE HAVE TO GRAB THE NEXT BOAT, WE'LL LOSE JONAH FOR GOOD!
BWAAAAAAAAA

JONAH WIZARD TAKING PUBLIC TRANSIT AND WALKING -- BOTH IN THE SAME DAY!
THE STRUGGLE IS REAL...
SHH, LOOK -- I THINK THEY'RE GOING INTO THAT STORE.
WHAT DO YOU THINK THEY'RE DOING IN THERE?
I DUNNO...
C'MON, AMY. LET'S TAKE A CLOSER LOOK.
SNEAK
SNEAK
SNEAK

A RECORD STORE? IS JONAH DOING A SIGNING TODAY OR SOMETHING?
I DON'T THINK SO... I MEAN, THEY HAVE POSTERS FOR ALL SORTS OF EVENTS, BUT THEY'RE NOT EVEN ADVERTISING THAT HE'S HERE.
WAIT... HE'S NOT HERE!
HUH? WHERE'D THEY GO??

WHAT'S GOING ON?
THEY'RE NOT IN THERE... JONAH AND HIS DAD JUST DISAPPEARED!
WHAT? BUT WE SAW THEM WALK IN!
HIS LAST NAME MAY BE *WIZARD,* BUT I *KNOW* HE CAN'T TELEPORT...
EXACTLY. EITHER JONAH AND HIS DAD ARE STILL IN THERE, OR THEY LEFT THROUGH A SECRET DOOR.
WE HAVE TO SEARCH THE STORE.
YEAH, DUH... BUT HOW DO WE DO THAT WITH A GUY AT THE CASH REGISTER?
OH NO... I DON'T LIKE WHERE *THIS* IS GOING...
NELLIE...
PLEASE HELP US, NELLIE. WE NEED A DIVERSION TO DRAW THE CLERK OUTSIDE.
WE'LL OWE YOU FOREVER... *PLEEEEEASE?*
OH BOY...

JINGLE
JANGLE
BUON POMERIGGIO... TI POSSO AIUTARE?
OH, I'M SORRY... I DON'T SPEAK ANY ITALIAN.
AH -- YOU ARE AMERICAN. I WILL ASSIST YOU. WHAT ARE YOU LOOKING FOR TODAY?
LET ME GUESS... YOU ENJOY PUNK MUSIC, PERHAPS?
MMM... MORE LIKE PUNK/ REGGAE FUSION. WITH A COUNTRY FEEL. AND OPERATIC VOCALS.
AH, SEE HERE? THIS IS PERFECT.
?
?
AND SOME OF THIS...AND THIS. OH, AND GOTTA HAVE *THIS.*

THERE WE GO! THAT SHOULD DO, FOR A START.
WELL, MISS... YOU ARE CLEARLY A MUSIC LOVER!
NO, NOT QUITE...
BUT I AM A KLEPTOMANIAC!
AH!
JINGLE JANGLE
Disco Volante
FERMATI! FERMATI!!

JINGLE JANGLE
OKAY...YOU CHECK BEHIND THE COUNTER, AND I'LL LOOK AROUND OUT HERE!
IT'S JUST AN OFFICE...
WITH NO WAY OUT!
RATTLE RATTLE
I THINK I FOUND SOMETHING OVER HERE! COME LOOK AT THIS.
WHAT IS THIS? A LISTENING BOOTH?
YEAH -- BUT DON'T YOU THINK THESE MUSICAL CHOICES ARE A LITTLE ODD?
THERE'S A LITTLE BIT OF EVERYTHING HERE... ROCK...ELECTRONICA... GRUNGE...SKA...
OH! AND *TWILIGHT OF GENIUS: THE LATER WORKS OF WOLFGANG AMADEUS MOZART!*

TWILIGHT OF GENIUS:
The Later Works
Wolfgang Am
Mozart
TWILIGHT OF GENIUS:
WELL, IT'S EXACTLY WHAT IT SAYS ON THE LABEL...MORE *MOZART!*
HANG ON...
SIDE A
Adagio für Harmon a
KV 356
SIDE B
Adagio and Rondo,
KV 617
MOZART
FLIP
CLUNK
WAHHHHH!!!

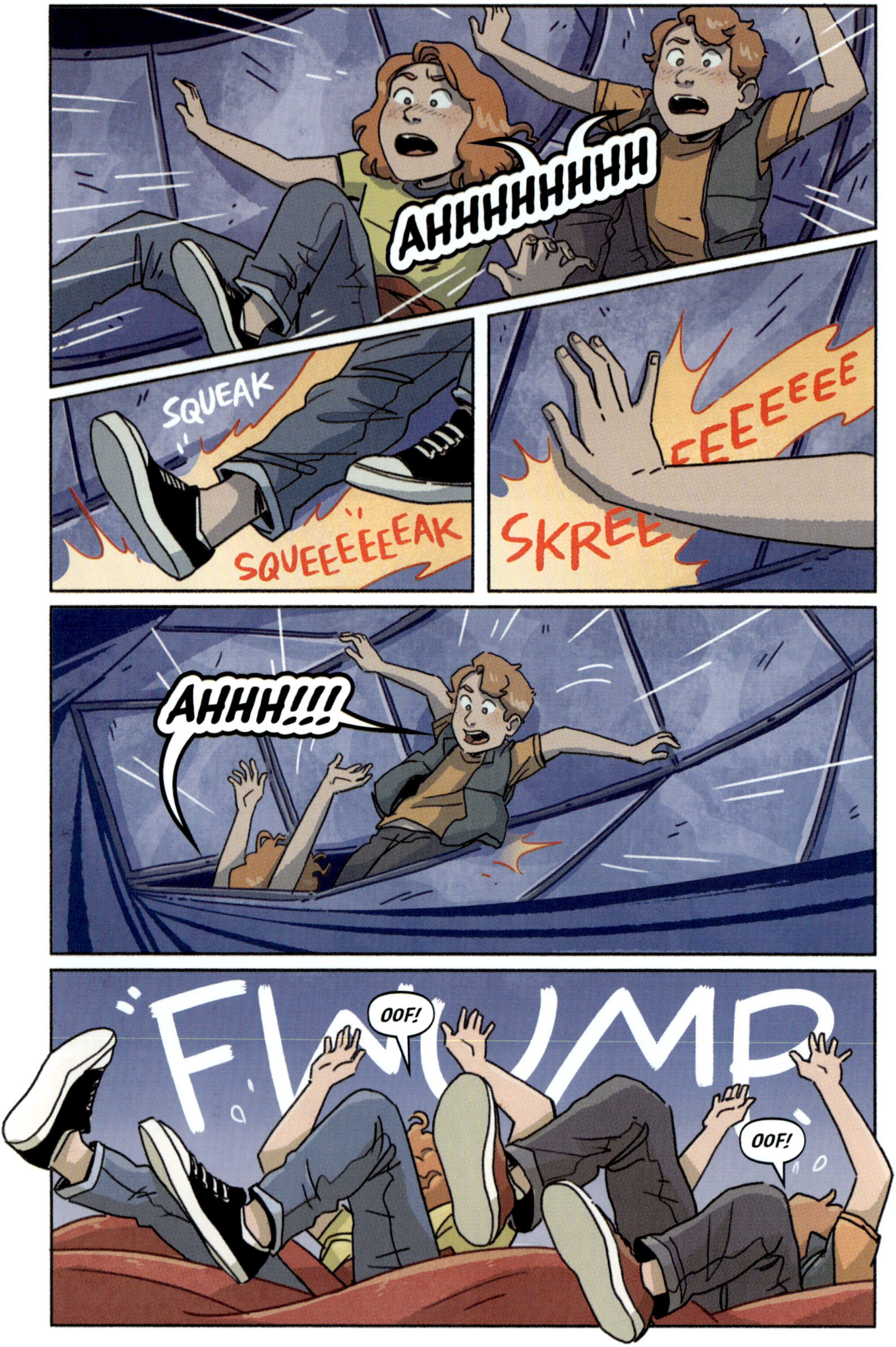
AHHHHHHHHH
SQUEAK
SQUEEEEEEAK
SKREEEEEEEEEE
AHHH!!!
FWUMP
OOF!
OOF!

A SECRET TRAPDOOR!
I GUESS THAT EXPLAINS WHERE JONAH AND HIS DAD WENT...
OH NO, I HEAR CLASSICAL MUSIC... ARE WE IN ANOTHER MOZART HOUSE?
I DON'T THINK SO...SOME OF THESE PAINTINGS ARE MODERN. IT LOOKS MORE LIKE AN ART MUSEUM.
AN UNDERGROUND MUSEUM WHERE YOU HAVE TO SLIDE DOWN FROM A RECORD STORE?
AND LOOK OVER HERE! I'M PRETTY SURE THIS IS A REMBRANDT.
YOU'RE TELLING ME THERE'S A MILLION-DOLLAR PAINTING AT THE BOTTOM OF A HOLE?
IF IT'S REAL, TRY FIFTY MILLION.
NO WAY! BUT THEN, ALL THIS MUST BE WORTH...
WELL, THERE ISN'T ENOUGH MONEY IN THE WORLD TO BUY HALF THIS STUFF!

HERE'S THE THING, THOUGH...GRACE WAS A REMBRANDT FANATIC.
SHE HAD TONS OF BOOKS OF HIS PAINTINGS, BUT I'VE NEVER SEEN THIS ONE BEFORE.
FAKE?
I DON'T THINK SO. THE STYLE IS PERFECT.
AND LOOK -- THAT'S DEFINITELY A PICASSO, BUT IT ISN'T FAMOUS, EITHER.
I THINK THIS MIGHT BE A SECRET GALLERY OF UNDISCOVERED MASTERPIECES!
WHAT WOULD THAT HAVE TO DO WITH JONAH WIZARD?
THAT WAS THE FINAL MOVEMENT OF THE UNFINISHED SYMPHONY BY OUR OWN FRANZ SCHUBERT.
YOU'RE LISTENING TO RADIO JANUS -- ALL JANUS, ALL THE TIME.
NEXT WE HAVE A ONE-OF-A-KIND RECORDING OF SCOTT JOPLIN PERFORMING AT HARRY HOUDINI'S BIRTHDAY PARTY.
JANUS! THAT'S ONE OF THE FOUR BRANCHES OF THE CAHILL FAMILY! THE JANUS, THE TOMAS, THE EKATERINA, AND THE LUCIAN!
I HATE LUCIANS! THAT'S THE KABRAS' BRANCH. IRINA, TOO--
REMEMBER WHEN SHE TOOK US TO THAT WEIRD COMMAND CENTER IN PARIS?
I THINK THIS MIGHT BE THE SAME KIND OF PLACE. ONLY THIS ONE'S FOR JANUS.
BUT WHO PUTS A COMMAND CENTER IN AN ART GALLERY?

WHAT IF EACH BRANCH OF THE FAMILY HAS A SPECIAL SKILL?
REMEMBER, THE FAMOUS LUCIANS WERE MOSTLY WORLD LEADERS, GREAT GENERALS, SECRET AGENTS, AND SPIES. WHAT DO THOSE CAREERS HAVE IN COMMON?
STRATEGY, PLOTTING -- MAYBE ***THAT'S*** THE LUCIAN TALENT!
SO YOU'RE SAYING THE JANUS ARE ARTISTS?
YES -- PEOPLE LIKE MOZART, A GREAT MUSICIAN. AND REMBRANDT AND PICASSO --
AND JONAH WIZARD! I MEAN, HE ***IS*** A BIG STAR.
EXACTLY... AND HE CAME HERE FOR A REASON!
WE HAVE TO FIGURE OUT WHAT HE'S AFTER AND GET TO IT FIRST.
AREN'T YOU FORGETTING SOMETHING?
JONAH'S A JANUS -- ***HE'S*** ALLOWED TO BE HERE, BUT WE'RE NOT.
GRACE NEVER TOLD US WHAT BRANCH WE BELONG TO... IT MIGHT BE JANUS.
I MEAN, ***I*** PLAY PIANO.
YEAH, BUT YOU'RE NO ***MOZART.*** AND ***I*** CAN'T DRAW A STRAIGHT LINE WITH A RULER.
FACE IT, AMY -- WE'RE ABOUT AS ARTISTIC AS A COUPLE OF HOCKEY PUCKS.

HMM...THIS IS WEIRD. IT'S LIKE WE'RE SPIRALING DEEPER AND DEEPER UNDERGROUND.
MAYBE THAT'S THE SHAPE OF THE STRONGHOLD... THEY DIDN'T HAVE A LOT OF SPACE, SO THEY DESIGNED THE PLACE LIKE A CORKSCREW.
IF THEY'VE GOT THE BEST ARTISTS, THEY'VE PROBABLY GOT THE BEST ARCHITECTS, TOO.
HOLY MOLY...
WHAT IS THAT? SOME KIND OF INSTALLATION ART?
NO WAY -- EVEN BETTER!
THIS IS THE ACTUAL NIEUPORT FIGHTER FLOWN BY RAOUL LUFBERY -- ONE OF THE GREATEST FLYING ACES OF WORLD WAR ONE!
BUT WAIT... I THOUGHT JANUS ARE SUPPOSED TO BE ARTISTS, NOT FIGHTER PILOTS.
I GUESS THAT DEPENDS ON WHAT YOU CALL AN ARTIST -- ARCHERY, TARGET SHOOTING, AERIAL COMBAT.
ON THE P.A. THEY WERE TALKING ABOUT HOUDINI, WHO WAS AN ESCAPE ARTIST.
MAN...THE JANUS GOT ALL THE COOLEST PEOPLE!
AND LOOK AT THIS!

WHERE SHOULD WE GO NEXT?
SCULPTURE... MOVIES...
B2 · PERMANENT COLLECTION
B3 · SCULPTURE
B4 · MOVIES
B5 · STRATEGIC PLANNING
B6 · INSTALLATIONS
B7 · OIL PAINTINGS
ERFORMANCE
EAPONS
STRATEGIC PLANNING?
WHY WOULD YOU NEED STRATEGIC PLANNING FOR AN ART MUSEUM?
IT'S NOT JUST A MUSEUM, REMEMBER?
IT'S A BASE OF OPERATIONS FOR THE WHOLE JANUS BRANCH TO PLAN STRATEGY.
PRESS
YEAH, BUT STRATEGY FOR WHAT?
WELL, FOR STARTERS, CLUE FINDING.
AW, COME ON!
THE CONTEST WAS ANNOUNCED AT GRACE'S FUNERAL.
NO WAY COULD THE JANUS BUILD A SETUP LIKE THIS IN TWO WEEKS.
THE OFFICIAL CONTEST BEGAN AT THE FUNERAL. THE CLUES HAVE BEEN AROUND SINCE MOZART'S TIME --
I'LL BET THE BRANCHES HAVE ALWAYS KNOWN ABOUT THE THIRTY-NINE CLUES.
DING
WUMMMMM
WAIT -- WE'RE MOVING, BUT WE DIDN'T PRESS A BUTTON YET!
OH NO! SOMEONE MUST HAVE CALLED THE ELEVATOR!
CLIK
CLIK
CLIK
CLIK
JUST HIT THE BUTTONS FOR AS MANY OTHER FLOORS AS YOU CAN! ONE OF THEM'S GOTTA COME FIRST!

DING
QUICK, BEHIND THE STATUE!

WHOA... WHAT PLANET ARE WE ON?

IT'S AMAZING... A WHOLE SOCIETY CELEBRATING ART AND CREATIVITY...
THIS MAKES ME HOPE WE SOMEHOW STILL TURN OUT TO BE JANUS.
THE PROBLEM IS... HOW DO WE GET PAST ALL THESE PEOPLE?
WHEN *YOU* GO TO A MOVIE, WHAT DO YOU PAY ATTENTION TO -- THE AUDIENCE OR THE SCREEN?
HUH? WHAT ARE YOU TALKING ABOUT?
WE CAN JUST BLEND INTO THE CROWD AND SLIP OUT THE OTHER SIDE!
DAN, NO, I CAN'T --

OOH!
BRAVO!
WOW!
CLAP
CLAP
CLAP CLAP
CLAP
CLAP
UDINI
UROSAWA
MOZART
EASY-PEASY! AND LOOK AT WHOSE NAME IS UP THERE!
NICE WORK.
COME ON -- THIS WAY.

MOZART
WOLFGANG
MARIA ANNA
LEOPOLD
WHO'S *LEOPOLD?*
THEIR FATHER. HE WAS A FAMOUS MUSICIAN IN HIS OWN RIGHT. HE DEVOTED HIS LIFE TO BRINGING OUT HIS KIDS' TALENTS -- ESPECIALLY WOLFGANG'S.
OH BOY...LOOK AT ALL THIS JUNK. THESE GUYS COULD *OUT-MOZART* THE MOZART HOUSES.
OH MY GOSH... EIGHTEENTH-CENTURY VIOLINS, WORTH A FORTUNE...
AN ORIGINAL COPY OF *VIOLIN METHOD,* THE NUMBER-ONE VIOLIN TEXTBOOK IN THE WORLD DURING THE 1700S...
OH, AND, DAN, LOOK -- IT'S THE HARPSICHORD MOZART PLAYED WHEN HE WAS THREE!
YAWN:

THINK ABOUT IT: YOU WERE STILL IN DIAPERS AT THAT AGE, AND HERE'S THIS TINY TODDLER PRESSING KEYS, LISTENING FOR "NOTES THAT LIKE EACH OTHER."
HEY, MAYBE MOZART WAS IN DIAPERS, TOO!
JUST BECAUSE HE WAS A GENIUS DOESN'T MEAN HE WAS ALREADY CHAMBER-POT-TRAINED.
HEY, WAIT A MINUTE... ISN'T THAT...?
THE MISSING PAGES!!

THESE ARE DEFINITELY THEM -- THE PAGES THAT WERE TORN OUT OF NANNERL'S DIARY!
WHAT DO THEY SAY?
WELL, THEY'RE IN GERMAN, LIKE THE REST OF THE DIARY...
WE HAVE TO GET THEM OUT OF HERE AND SHOW THEM TO NELLIE.
THAT MIGHT BE TRICKY... I'M PRETTY SURE THAT'S A RETINAL SCANNER.
YOU HAVE TO STICK YOUR CHIN IN THE HOLDER, AND THE LIGHT READS YOUR EYEBALLS.
IT'S WORTH A TRY... MAYBE OUR EYEBALLS WILL PASS.
FOUR BRANCHES OF THE FAMILY -- A ONE-IN-FOUR CHANCE WE'VE GOT JANUS RETINAS...
THIS PLACE IS WILD! MOM NEVER TOLD ME ALL THESE HEAVY HITTERS WERE CAHILLS!
JONAH!
IT IS IMPRESSIVE. CLEARLY, THE JANUS NAME MADE A GREATER CONTRIBUTION TO THE ARTS THAN ANY FAMILY IN HUMAN HISTORY.
QUICK -- BEHIND THE HARPSICHORD!

HERE'S A PIECE THAT WILL BE OF SPECIAL INTEREST TO AN AMERICAN...
PERHAPS THE MOST WIDELY COPIED PICTURE OF ALL TIME --
THE PORTRAIT OF YOUR FIRST PRESIDENT, GEORGE WASHINGTON, PRINTED ON EVERY U.S. DOLLAR BILL FOR MORE THAN A CENTURY, AND PAINTED IN 1796 BY GILBERT STUART...
A CAHILL.
BUT I THOUGHT THAT PICTURE WAS IN THE MUSEUM OF FINE ARTS IN BOSTON?
THAT IS JUST THE ROUGH DRAFT. MOST OF THE CANVAS IS LEFT BLANK. THIS PIECE IS --
WHAT DO YOU AMERICANS CALL IT?
THE REAL DEAL?
ESATTAMENTE. MOST JANUS ARTISTS RESERVE THEIR VERY BEST FOR US.
NOW, IF YOU'LL FOLLOW ME...
THIS IS, I BELIEVE, WHAT YOU CAME FOR...FROM THE JOURNAL OF MARIA ANNA MOZART.
SERIOUS SECURITY. THESE PAPERS MUST BE IMPORTANT, HUH?
JONAH DOESN'T DO RETINAL SCANS.
HIS EYES ARE INSURED WITH LLOYD'S OF LONDON FOR ELEVEN MILLION DOLLARS --
CHILL OUT, DAD. ONE TIME WON'T HURT.

CONFIRMATION COMPLETE -- WIZARD, JONAH; MOTHER: CORA WIZARD, MEMBER, JANUS HIGH COUNCIL;
FATHER: BRODERICK T. WIZARD, NON-CAHILL, LIMITED JANUS AUTHORIZATION.
WHIRR-CLICK
HMPH.
YOU'LL REVIEW THE PAGES IN OUR OFFICE, OF COURSE.
NATURALLY, WE CAN'T ALLOW THEM TO LEAVE THE STRONGHOLD.
I'M SURE MY WIFE WILL BE INTERESTED TO KNOW HOW YOU RUN THIS PLACE LIKE AN ARMED CAMP...EVEN FOR HER OWN **SON.**
YOUR **WIFE** DESIGNED OUR SECURITY PROTOCOLS PERSONALLY.
AMY, STOP!
WHAT ARE YOU GOING TO DO? MUG JONAH WIZARD IN THE MIDDLE OF JANUS HEADQUARTERS?
WE CAN'T LET HIM GO! WE MIGHT AS WELL JUST HAND HIM THE WHOLE CONTEST!
GETTING YOURSELF CAUGHT ISN'T GOING TO CHANGE THAT!
WE'D HAVE TO FIGHT A GANG OF CRAZY ARTISTS WHO'D RIP OUR HEADS OFF FOR THOSE PAGES.
YOU'RE RIGHT! THEY'LL DO **ANYTHING** TO PROTECT THEIR ARTWORK!
COME ON!

RIGHT THIS WAY, SIRS...
IT'S NOW OR NEVER!
HOLD UP -- ISN'T THAT -- ?
GRAB
AMY CAHILL?!
NO! STOP!!!
FREEZE!
ONE MORE STEP AND GEORGE GETS A FACE FULL OF PAINT!
YOU WOULDN'T DARE!
ARE YOU KIDDING? THAT'S MY SISTER! SHE'S ON THE EDGE!

WHAT DO YOU CAHILLS WANT?
THOSE PAPERS YOU'RE TRYING TO HIDE. HAND THEM OVER.
OH, *THESE?* JUST GARBAGE --
I WAS GONNA LOOK FOR A TRASH CAN ON MY WAY OUT.
COUGH 'EM UP, *WIZARD!*
I'M NOT AFRAID TO USE THIS!
YOU'RE BLUFFING!
SLIME HIM, SIS.
NO-O!
YOU CAN HAVE THE PAGES! JUST DON'T HARM THAT PICTURE!

YOU DON'T HAVE THAT AUTHORITY!
THERE'S A LOT MORE AT STAKE HERE THAN A PAINTING!
YOU ARE NOT A JANUS, SIR!
YOU WILL NEVER APPRECIATE THE UNIQUE AND IRREPLACEABLE LIFE FORCE IN ANY WORK OF ART --
LET ALONE A PRICELESS MASTERPIECE!
LAST CHANCE!
PLEASE... YOU UNDERSTAND, DON'T YOU, YOUNG MAN?
Y-YOU TAKE AFTER YOUR MOTHER... SHE WOULD NEVER ALLOW THIS PORTRAIT TO BE RUINED, DON'T YOU AGREE?
NOD
NOD
GOOSH
YOINK
HEY!
THEY TOOK THE PAGES!
DON'T WORRY... THEY WON'T GET FAR.

BWAMP-BWAMP-BWA
SHOULDN'T WE BE GOING UP, NOT DOWN?
STAIRS! THERE!
WAMP-BWAMP-BWA
YOU'LL NEVER MAKE IT, YOU GUYS!
COME BACK AND WE CAN WORK SOMETHING OUT!
C'MON, KIDS -- NOWHERE TO GO!
DONK
ACK!
OUCH!
BONK
CLANG
ARGH!
OOF!
PUSH
CLONG

WHERE ARE WE? ANY IDEA HOW TO GET BACK TO THE RECORD STORE??
THERE MUST BE A DIFFERENT EXIT!
OH NO... NO MORE STAIRS!
WHAT'S THIS WEIRD METAL BOX? IS THIS A DOOR?
I DON'T SEE A HANDLE.
I THINK WE'RE TRAPPED!
UP HERE! THIS WAY!

TOLD YOU GUYS --
NO WAY OUT.
GOT ANY MORE
MIRACLES?
WAIT --
ABOVE US!
I THINK THAT'S
A SHUTTER!
AIRLOCK
PUMP OFF
PUMP ON
NO!!
KERCLUNK

SIX

SLAM
WUMMMMMMM
SLOSH
AIRLOCK
PUMP OFF
PUMP ON
WUMMMMMMMM
GURGLE
GURGLE
THAT'S OUR WAY OUT!
BUT WHERE DID THE WATER COME FROM?!
ARE YOU KIDDING ME?
WE'RE IN VENICE -- WITH ALL THE CANALS, REMEMBER?
KSHHHHHHHHHHH
GURGLE
GURGLE
NOW CLIMB!

WHOA! IT'S LIKE THE WATER IS THE ROAD, AND PEOPLE DRIVE BOATS INSTEAD OF CARS.
YEAH, APPARENTLY SOME VENETIANS HARDLY EVER SET FOOT ON THE STREET.
THEY CAN GET EVERYWHERE THEY NEED TO GO ON THE CANALS...
WE BETTER GET MOVING... IT WON'T TAKE LONG FOR THEM TO RESET THAT AIRLOCK.
AH! DAN -- STOP!

WE'RE TRAPPED!
I GUESS THE ONLY OTHER WAY TO GET TO THIS DOCK MUST BE BY BOAT...
SO WHAT DO WE DO NOW?
DAN, NO! THAT'S STEALING!
HOP
IT'S BORROWING -- THIS IS AN EMERGENCY!
HEY!

DAN!!
HANG ON!
VMMM
ZMMMMM
ZOOM

DAN, THIS IS CRAZY! YOU CAN'T DRIVE A BOAT!
OH YEAH? THEN WHAT AM I DOING RIGHT N--
BONK
AHHHHH!!!
DAN, BE CAREFUL!!!
SORRY, SORRY... EYES ON THE ROAD --
ER, I MEAN, *CANAL.*

LISTEN, WE HAVE TO PROTECT THE DIARY PAGES, IN CASE JONAH CATCHES UP TO US.
WE SHOULD DITCH THEM FOR A LITTLE WHILE, JUST UNTIL THE COAST IS CLEAR.
ZMMMMMM
DITCH THEM? WE NEARLY GOT KILLED BREAKING THEM OUT OF THE STRONGHOLD!
THAT'S WHY WE HAVE TO STASH THEM IN A VERY SAFE PLACE. THEN WE'LL COME BACK FOR THEM ONCE WE'RE SURE NO ONE IS FOLLOWING US.
BUT WE DON'T KNOW VENICE! IF WE HIDE THOSE PAGES, WE MIGHT NEVER FIND THEM AGAIN!
ALL THE MORE REASON TO FIND A PLACE THAT'S IMPOSSIBLE TO FORGET...
Royal Saladin

MAKE SURE OUR BOAT DOESN'T DRIFT -- I'M GONNA FIND A HIDING SPOT!
PICK SOMEWHERE DRY! IF THE PAPERS GET WET, THEY'LL BE RUINED.
ZIP
OKAY, GREAT JOB -- COME ON!
HOP

OKAY, YOU'RE THE EXPERT.
WHERE SHOULD WE GO TO KILL TIME, AMY?
LET'S FIND THE GRAND CANAL! IT'S THE MOST FAMOUS CANAL IN VENICE, AND THE BIGGEST --
WE'RE SURE TO BLEND IN WITH ALL THE OTHER BOATS OUT THERE!
GOT IT... SO HOW DO WE GET THERE?
JUST FOLLOW THE MAIN WATERWAYS! THEY MUST ALL CONNECT EVENTUALLY.
THERE! TAKE A LEFT --
I THINK THAT'S IT!
WHOA... THAT CANAL DOES LOOK HUGE!

INCREDIBLE!
LOOK AT ALL THIS! DELIVERY BOATS, POLICE BOATS, GARBAGE BOATS... THEY HAVE A BOAT FOR EVERYTHING!
OH -- AND DAN, LOOK OVER THERE!
I THINK THAT'S THE PONTE DI RIALTO -- ONE OF THE MOST FAMOUS BRIDGES IN THE WORLD!
WOW...
HEY, I THINK I'M GETTING PRETTY GOOD AT THIS. I COULD BE A PROFESSIONAL BOAT...GUY.
IS THAT A THING?
SURE, DAN, WHATEVER YOU --
HUH?
UH-OH...

IT'S HEADED RIGHT FOR US!
TURN THE BOAT! TURN THE BOAT!
I'M TRYING, I'M TRYING!
BUT THEY'RE TURNING *INTO* US!!
THEY'RE CRAZY!
HANG ON!!!
CCCRRONCH

WHERE...ARE WE?
MOM AND DAD'S FUNERAL?
IMPOSSIBLE...
NO...THIS ISN'T REAL.
WAKE UP. WAKE UP!
WAKE UP! AMY, WAKE UP!

GUH!
WHERE ARE WE?
I THINK WE'RE ON THE YACHT.
THE DOOR'S LOCKED.
I HEARD VOICES OUTSIDE EARLIER, BUT I DON'T THINK JONAH WAS ONE OF THEM.
I'VE GOT A BAD FEELING ABOUT THIS, DAN.
WHAT IF WE ESCAPED FROM THE JANUS ONLY TO GET CAUGHT BY SOMEBODY EVEN WORSE?
WORSE?
DO YOU THINK THEY COULD BE... MADRIGALS?
WHAT DO YOU KNOW ABOUT THE MADRIGALS?

THE *KABRAS!*
WE SHOULD'VE GUESSED.
NO ONE UNDERSTANDS THE MADRIGALS.
NO ONE'S EVEN SURE WHO THEY ARE.
NO ONE EXCEPT GRACE!
AND SHE TOLD *US!*
LIAR!
TOUCHY... I GUESS YOU DON'T LIKE IT WHEN SOMEBODY KNOWS SOMETHING YOU DON'T.
OUR PARENTS TELL US EVERYTHING!
NOT LIKE YOUR PRECIOUS GRACE, WHO LEFT YOU IN THE DARK AND THEN TURNED YOU LOOSE TO WRECK THE CONTEST!
CALM DOWN, IAN, HE'S JUST TRYING TO GET TO YOU.

WHAT DO YOU WANT?
ONLY WHAT YOU STOLE FROM THE JANUS STRONGHOLD.
WE DON'T KNOW WHAT YOU'RE TALKING ABOUT.
DON'T PLAY DUMB.
WE KNOW THE STRONGHOLD IS HERE -- WE HAVE SURVEILLANCE CAMERAS ALL OVER VENICE.
WELL, OKAY... WE WERE IN THE STRONGHOLD -- BUT WE DIDN'T TAKE ANYTHING!
YEAH!
SEARCH US IF YOU DON'T BELIEVE IT.
AS IF WE HADN'T ALREADY DONE THAT.
THE TWO OF YOU MAKE ME SICK... YOU LOOK LIKE YOU CRAWLED OUT OF A SEWER.
WE DID CRAWL OUT OF A SEWER!
IT'S TOO BAD YOU WORMED YOUR WAY OUT OF THAT TUNNEL EXPLOSION IN SALZBURG.
YOU WOULD'VE DONE THE WORLD A FAVOR BY STAYING DOWN THERE...FOREVER.
THAT WAS YOU?!

YOU THINK IT WAS **HARD** TO FOOL ALISTAIR INTO THINKING HE WAS OUR ALLY?
WE SHOULD HAVE GIVEN THE OLD STICK INSECT A BIGGER BOMB. THEN WE'D BE RID OF THE LOT OF YOU.
FORGET IT, IAN. CLEARLY, THEY HAVE NOTHING.
CAPTAIN!
YES, MISS?
THESE STOWAWAYS NEED TO PUT OFF THE SHIP.
WE DIDN'T **STOW AWAY!**
YOU SUNK OUR BOAT AND PULLED US OUT OF THE CANAL!
GOOD POINT. RETURN THEM TO THE CANAL.
ROUGHLY, PLEASE.

COME ON, MISTER -- GIVE US A BREAK!
I HAVE MY ORDERS.
SPLASH
GASP
"COUGH
SPLUTTER"

SPLISH SPLASH SPLISH SPLASH
YOU OKAY, AMY?
SPLOOSH
GOOSH
YEAH, I THINK SO...JUST SOAKED TO THE BONE.
WE SHOULD GO GET THOSE PAGES.
SHAKE
SHAKE
WRING
OKAY, BUT FIRST LET'S FIND NELLIE.
IT'S GETTING LATE AND WE NEED AN ADULT...AND DRY CLOTHES.
WUMMMMM
A GRENADE LAUNCHER WOULD BE NICE, TOO.

OUTSIDE DISCO VOLANTE...
OHHH... HOW COULD I BE SO STUPID?
I SHOULD NEVER HAVE LET THEM RUN OFF BY THEMSELVES AGAIN.
WHERE ARE THEY, SALADIN? HOW DO TWO KIDS GO INTO A MUSIC STORE AND NEVER COME OUT?
MRRP.
THAT'S EASY FOR YOU TO SAY... YOU'RE NOT IN CHARGE OF THOSE TWO LITTLE GREMLINS.
OKAY. THAT'S IT.
IT'S BEEN FOUR HOURS -- I'M BREAKING IN.
MRUH?!
GRAB
HERE GOES NOTHING --
NELLIE?

KIDS!!!
OH, THANK GOODNESS YOU'RE OKAY!
I AM NEVER LETTING YOU OUT OF MY SIGHT AGAIN, YOU HEAR --
YUCK -- WHY ARE YOU ALL WET?
IT'S A LONG STORY...BUT RIGHT NOW WE NEED TO GO PICK SOMETHING UP.
WE'LL EXPLAIN ON THE WAY.
COME ON.

ONE EXPLANATION LATER...
...AND SO THE BOAT WHERE WE HID THE PAGES SHOULD BE RIGHT...
...HERE.
OH NO...
OH, GREAT... WHO HAS A PARTY ON A BOAT?
NOT A PARTY... A WEDDING!
Royal Saladin
YOU'RE TELLING ME THE PAGES YOU RISKED YOUR LIVES FOR ARE PROBABLY UNDERNEATH A WEDDING GUEST'S BUTT RIGHT NOW?
IT'S OKAY... WE'LL JUST DO WHAT WE DID AT THE BASE EARLIER.
AMY AND I CAN BLEND INTO THE CROWD AND --
NOT SO FAST.

IF YOU THINK I'M LETTING YOU GO OFF ON YOUR OWN AFTER THESE STUPID PAGES **ONE MORE TIME,** YOU'RE OUT OF YOUR MINDS.
BUT --
NO BUTS.
BUT, NELLIE, THOSE PAGES ARE OUR ONLY CLUE!
IF WE GIVE UP NOW, EVERYTHING WILL HAVE BEEN A WASTE --
WAIT...
WHAT ARE YOU DOING?
YOU TWO HAVE HAD A LONG DAY...
WHY DON'T YOU LET A PRO TAKE CARE OF THIS ONE.
BESIDES, YOU LOOK LIKE A COUPLE OF DROWNED RATS --
YOU'D STICK OUT LIKE SORE THUMBS AT A WEDDING.

WHAT IS SHE *DOING?!* SHE'S JUST WALKING RIGHT UP THERE!
SHE'S NUTS! SHE DOESN'T EVEN SPEAK ITALIAN!
FINGER-GUNS?
OH MY GOD...
I GUESS SOME THINGS ARE UNIVERSAL.
YOINK
CLINK
ol Saladin
AND NOW SHE'S...
...DANCING?!

WAIT, DAN, LOOK!
I THINK SHE'S ASKING WHICH CUSHION YOU HID THE PAGES IN!
NOT THAT ONE!
THE ONE RIGHT NEXT TO YOU!!!
WOW, LOOK AT HER GO...
SHE MUST REALLY LOVE US, HUH?
STUFF
STUFF
WE HAVE THE COOLEST AU PAIR EVER.
YEAH.
WE'RE PRETTY LUCKY.
GO! QUICK, BEFORE THEY REALIZE!
HEE
HEE
HEE
HEE
HEE
HEE
HEE

SEVEN

THE NEXT DAY...
WELL, YOU'RE NOT GOING TO BELIEVE THIS, YOU GUYS...IT'S NO WONDER SOMEBODY RIPPED THESE PAGES OUT.
THEY'RE ALL ABOUT HOW WORRIED NANNERL WAS -- SHE THOUGHT MOZART WAS GOING *CRAZY.*
CRAZY?
YOU MEAN, LIKE, BEYOND DEVOTING HIS LIFE TO THIS BORING MUSIC?
HE WAS RUNNING HIMSELF INTO MAJOR DEBT -- BUT THE STUFF HE WAS BUYING WAS POINTLESS AND WEIRD.
HE WAS IMPORTING RARE AND EXPENSIVE INGREDIENTS FROM OVERSEAS.
I BET THIS MUST BE CONNECTED TO THE THIRTY-NINE CLUES SOMEHOW.
MOZART WAS IN IT UP TO HIS EARS. JUST LIKE BEN FRANKLIN.
THE DIARY MENTIONS FRANKLIN, TOO -- RIGHT HERE.
AND YOU'LL NEVER GUESS WHO ELSE WAS A CAHILL --
...MARIE ANTOINETTE? WE'RE RELATED TO THE ***QUEEN OF FRANCE?!***
AND THE AUSTRIAN ROYAL FAMILY, TOO. THAT WAS THE CONNECTION --
WHEN SHE MARRIED THE FUTURE KING LOUIS XVI AND WENT TO FRANCE, SHE BECAME THE GO-BETWEEN FOR FRANKLIN AND MOZART.

BUT THERE'S SOMETHING ELSE YOU SHOULD SEE... A NOTE IN THE MARGIN HERE.
THAT'S --
GRACE WROTE THIS! I'D KNOW THAT HANDWRITING ANYWHERE...
THE WORD THAT COST HER LIFE, MINUS THE MUSIC.
The word that cost her life, minus the music.
WHY DOES EVERYTHING HAVE TO BE A PUZZLE WITH YOU CAHILLS...WHY CAN'T YOU JUST SAY WHAT YOU MEAN?
THEN IT WOULDN'T BE THE THIRTY-NINE CLUES --
IT WOULD BE THE THIRTY-NINE STATEMENTS.
THE THING MARIE ANTOINETTE WAS MOST FAMOUS FOR...
WHEN SOMEONE TOLD HER THE PEASANTS WERE RIOTING BECAUSE THERE WAS NO BREAD, SHE SAID, "LET THEM EAT CAKE."
YOU CAN GET FAMOUS FOR THAT?
DON'T YOU SEE? THERE WAS NO CAKE! THERE WAS NO FOOD AT ALL!
THOSE WORDS HELPED SET OFF THE FRENCH REVOLUTION...AND THAT WAS WHEN MARIE ANTOINETTE DIED BY THE GUILLOTINE!

SO YOU'RE SAYING THAT THE WORD THAT COST HER LIFE WAS... CAKE?
"MINUS THE MUSIC"... WHAT COULD THAT MEAN?
WELL, MARIE ANTOINETTE SPOKE FRENCH, SO --
WAIT A MINUTE! I KNOW THIS!
GRACE TOLD ME ABOUT IT WHEN I WAS A LITTLE KID!
HOW COME YOU CAN ALWAYS DREDGE UP SOME WEIRD GRACE CONVERSATION FROM A MILLION YEARS AGO?
WE KNEW HER AS A COOL GRANDMOTHER, BUT ALL THOSE YEARS, I THINK SHE WAS TRAINING US FOR THIS CONTEST --
PLANTING PIECES OF INFORMATION THAT WE WERE GOING TO NEED. THIS MIGHT BE ONE OF THEM.
AND WHAT IS "THIS"?
WHEN MARIE ANTOINETTE SAID, "LET THEM EAT CAKE," SHE'S USUALLY QUOTED USING THE FRENCH WORD BRIOCHE.
BUT GRACE WAS VERY CAREFUL TO TELL ME THAT SHE USED THE MORE COMMON TERM FOR CAKE -- GATEAU.
SO WHAT? CAKE IS CAKE, ISN'T IT?
UNLESS THIS HAD NOTHING TO DO WITH CAKE.
MARIE ANTOINETTE REALLY WAS SENDING SECRET MESSAGES BETWEEN FRANKLIN AND MOZART... MAYBE IT'S SOME KIND OF CODE.
HEY, AMY, LOOK! THERE'S ANOTHER NOTE --
I THINK GRACE WROTE IT, TOO!

D>HIC...?
MAYBE SHE HAD THE HICCUPS?
WAIT -- THE MARKINGS ARE RIGHT OVER A NAME...
D>HIC
fidelio Racco
FIDELIO RACCO.
THAT'S THE GUY ON UNCLE ALISTAIR'S PAPER!
MOZART PERFORMED AT THAT GUY'S HOUSE!
IT SAYS HERE HE WAS A BIG-TIME MERCHANT, AND MOZART HIRED HIM TO IMPORT SOME SUPER-EXPENSIVE KIND OF STEEL.
NANNERL BLAMES RACCO FOR OVERCHARGING HER BROTHER AND LANDING HIM IN DEBT.
AND GUESS WHAT SHE CALLS HIM?
COUSIN.
ANOTHER CAHILL?!
WELL...LET'S SEE WHAT WE CAN LEARN ABOUT OUR ITALIAN RELATIVE.

SO WE'RE LOOKING FOR COLLEZIONE DI RACCO... IT SHOULD BE ONLY A FEW MINUTES' WALK FROM HERE.
APPARENTLY IT CONTAINS ALL THE TREASURES AND ARTWORK HE COLLECTED ON HIS WORLD TRAVELS!
DID YOU KNOW HE WAS A MULTIMILLIONAIRE? AND IN HIS TIME, THAT WAS WORTH A LOT MORE!
INTERESTING THAT MOZART STILL ENDED UP MORE FAMOUS...
I GUESS IT GOES TO SHOW THAT MONEY ISN'T EVERYTHING.
SOMEONE SHOULD TELL THAT TO THE KABRAS...
THIS MUST BE IT! THAT'S RACCO'S STATUE!
HE'S PLAYING AN INSTRUMENT... ANOTHER JANUS?
THAT WOULD EXPLAIN WHY MOZART CAME TO HIM TO IMPORT THAT SPECIAL STEEL.
HE FIGURED HE'D BE SAFE WITH SOMEONE FROM HIS OWN BRANCH.
BAD MOVE, WOLFGANG... NEVER TRUST A CAHILL.

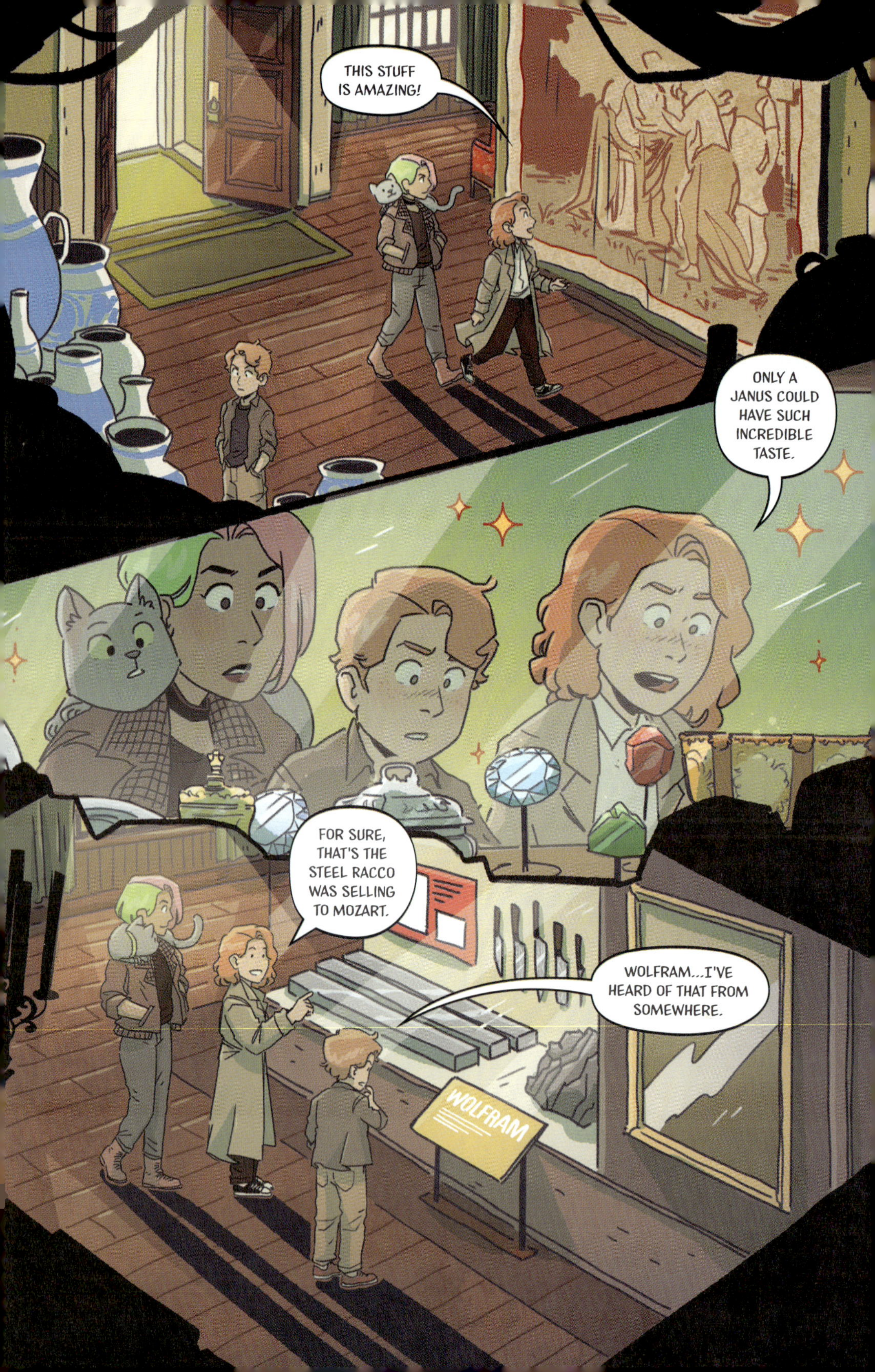
THIS STUFF IS AMAZING!
ONLY A JANUS COULD HAVE SUCH INCREDIBLE TASTE.
FOR SURE, THAT'S THE STEEL RACCO WAS SELLING TO MOZART.
WOLFRAM...I'VE HEARD OF THAT FROM SOMEWHERE.
WOLFRAM

ARE YOU SURE YOU'RE NOT THINKING OF **WOLFGANG?**
NO, **WOLFRAM.** GRACE TOLD ME ABOUT IT.
YOU'RE NOT THE ONLY GRANDCHILD SHE TOLD STUFF TO, YOU KNOW.
ALL RIGHT, WHAT DID SHE SAY?
WELL...I WAS SORT OF TUNING HER OUT.
TYPICAL. THAT'S WHY SHE TOLD MOST OF IT TO **ME** -- BECAUSE SHE KNEW YOU'D FORGET IT ALL.

OH NO, I'M OUT OF HERE! THIS IS STARTING TO LOOK A LOT LIKE YOU-KNOW-WHO...
IT IS YOU-KNOW-WHO! IT SAYS RIGHT HERE --
THIS IS THE INSTRUMENT MOZART PLAYED AT HIS PERFORMANCE IN RACCO'S HOUSE IN 1770!
THERE'S ONLY ONE PROBLEM: IT'S A HARPSICHORD.
IT DOESN'T TELL US WHAT D>HIC MEANS, AND IT HAS NOTHING TO DO WITH CAKE.
STILL...EVERYTHING WE'VE BEEN THROUGH HAS BEEN LEADING US TO THIS INSTRUMENT.
IT'S GOING TO GIVE US THE NEXT CLUE. I'M SURE OF IT.
DAN...DO YOU STILL HAVE THAT SHEET MUSIC YOU COPIED DOWN?
OH YEAH! HANG ON...
OF COURSE! WE TAKE A MUSICAL CLUE FROM BEN FRANKLIN AND PLAY IT ON MOZART'S INSTRUMENT!

WELL, WE CAN'T DO IT NOW...THAT GUY WOULD BEAT OUR HEADS IN IF WE LAID A FINGER ON HIS PRECIOUS KEYBOARD.
GOOD POINT.
THE HOUSE CLOSES AT FIVE. WE'RE GOING TO HAVE TO HIDE OUT TILL THEN.
HE'S RIGHT, NELLIE...WHY DON'T YOU AND SALADIN HEAD BACK OUT AND --
OH NO, NO, NO...
WE'RE NOT SPLITTING UP AGAIN -- LOOK WHAT HAPPENED YESTERDAY!
WE KNOW IT'S DANGEROUS...
BUT DAN AND I ARE THE ONLY ONES SMALL ENOUGH TO FIND A HIDING SPOT UNTIL AFTER-HOURS.
BESIDES, SALADIN HAS BARELY EATEN FOR DAYS NOW... HE REALLY NEEDS A GOOD MEAL.
MAYBE YOU CAN GO SHOPPING AND FIND SOMETHING HE'LL ACTUALLY TRY...
MROWR.
TRUST US, NELLIE. THIS IS OUR HUNT, OUR CLUES, OUR FAMILY.
WE CAN DO THIS.
OKAY.
BUT PLEASE... BE CAREFUL.

IT WAS A SMART IDEA TO HIDE OUT IN THESE BATHROOMS -- I GUESS AMY'S BRAIN COMES IN HANDY EVERY *ONCE* IN A WHILE.
WHAT A NERD...
I BET SHE'S THINKING ABOUT THE TILE IN HERE OR SOMETHING BORING LIKE THAT...
JUST A LITTLE LONGER UNTIL IT'S SAFE TO COME OUT.
WE'RE GETTING CLOSE TO SOMETHING BIG...I CAN FEEL IT.
THIS IS ALL SO WILD... AND TO FIND OUT WE'RE RELATED TO ROYALTY! AS WELL AS A BUNCH OF CON ARTISTS...
I WONDER IF MOM AND DAD KNEW ALL THIS...WERE THEY CON ARTISTS, TOO?
I MISS THEM.

I'M SO GLAD DAN IS BRAVE... I WOULDN'T EXPERIENCE HALF THE COOL STUFF I HAVE WITHOUT HIS ENCOURAGEMENT. EVEN THIS BEAUTIFUL BATHROOM...
I WONDER IF THE TILE IN HERE IS ART DECO...
AND I WONDER WHAT WILL BE WAITING FOR US OUT THERE WHEN WE PLAY THAT HARPSICHORD.
GOSH, THIS ADVENTURE HAS BEEN SO CRAZY...
EXPLOSIONS, BOAT CHASES, AND NOW BREAKING INTO A MUSEUM...
IT FEELS MORE LIKE A REALITY SHOW.
BUT REAL PEOPLE GETTING HURT... THAT'S NO GAME.
AND THE FIRE THAT KILLED MOM AND DAD...
THE MORE I THINK ABOUT IT...WAS IT REALLY ACCIDENTAL?
I MISS THEM.

WELL, I KNOW ONE THING FOR SURE: THEY WOULDN'T WANT US TO GIVE UP.
WE HAVE TO DO THIS FOR THEM.
WE OWE IT TO MOM AND DAD...
TO FIND THE TRUTH.

AMY? YOU READY?
YEAH. IT LOOKS LIKE THE COAST IS CLEAR...
LET'S GO.
SNEAK
SNEAK
THIS IS IT...
WE'RE GETTING SO CLOSE... I CAN FEEL IT!
GOOD EVENING, COUSINS.

WE HAVE **GOT** TO STOP MEETING LIKE THIS.
CLICK
NOT SO FAST, **DANNY BOY.**
GRAB
WHAT DO YOU WANT?
BASICALLY, IT'S LIKE THIS: YOU'RE GOING TO STAND IN FRONT OF MY SISTER'S DART GUN WHILE I ENTERTAIN YOU WITH SOME MUSIC.
DON'T WORRY -- THE DART WON'T KILL YOU.
BUT YOU'LL WAKE UP IN A FEW HOURS WITH A NASTY HEADACHE.
CRICK CRACK
YOU'RE BLUFFING! YOU DON'T EVEN KNOW WHAT TO PLAY!

I'M SURE SOMETHING WILL COME TO ME. PERHAPS "THREE BLIND MICE." OR "POP GOES THE WEASEL." OR MAYBE A LITTLE TUNE CALLED...
KV 617.
HOW COULD YOU KNOW ABOUT THAT?
YOU THINK YOU'RE SO CLEVER, BUT REALLY, YOU'RE PATHETIC.
WE INTERCEPTED YOUR PHONE'S WIRELESS SIGNAL -- YOU DOWNLOADED THIS PIECE, AND WE DOWNLOADED IT FROM YOU.
YOU CAN'T HIDE ANYTHING FROM US...
WE HAVE ***ALL THE SAME INFORMATION*** YOU DO.
AH, WHAT A MAGNIFICENT INSTRUMENT.
WAIT... WHAT'S THAT?
A WIRE...

CONNECTED TO... D ABOVE HIGH C.
D>HIC
GRACE'S NOTE ON THE NANNERL PAGES! IT'S A WARNING!
THAT D KEY IS BOOBY-TRAPPED!
DON'T!
CLICK
STOP!!!
BLAM!
PING

KABOOM

ZIP
Z
Z
Z

AMY!
ARE YOU
OKAY?
QUICK! THE
MUSIC!
IT'S NOT GOING
TO PLAY NOW!
IT'S ON FIRE!
CLICK
MAYBE SO,
BUT THE WIRES ARE
STILL CONNECTED.
CLICK
CLICK
CLICK
CLICK
KERCHUNK

NOW YOU'VE DONE IT! THE WHOLE BUILDING'S COMING DOWN!
RUMBLE
HUH?
KLUNK
ZMMMMMMMMMMM
WHOA! SAMURAI!
SAMURAI WARRIORS CARRIED TWO BLADES -- ONE SHORT AND ONE LONG.
THESE MUST BE THE SHORT ONES. SERIOUSLY COOL.
AND I'LL BET THEY'RE MADE WITH THAT SPECIAL STEEL MOZART WAS INTERESTED IN.
BUT HOW CAN THAT BE OUR CLUE? IT HAS NOTHING TO DO WITH THE STUFF GRACE WROTE IN THOSE DIARY PAGES.

D ABOVE HIGH C TURNED OUT TO BE THE BOOBY-TRAPPED HARPSICHORD KEY.
AND *GATEAU* MINUS THE MUSIC...
MUSICAL NOTES ARE ALSO LETTERS, REMEMBER? **A, B, C, D, E, F, AND G.**
IF YOU TAKE THOSE OUT OF THE WORD GATEAU, YOU'RE LEFT WITH... **T-U.**
THE OLD CHEMICAL SYMBOL FOR TUNGSTEN! **THAT'S** THE THING GRACE TOLD ME THAT I FORGOT!
WOLFRAM IS WHAT THEY USED TO CALL TUNGSTEN!
THAT'S WHY MARIE ANTOINETTE SAID, "LET THEM EAT CAKE." SHE WASN'T TALKING ABOUT THE **POOR** --
GATEAU WAS THE CODED MESSAGE BETWEEN FRANKLIN AND MOZART TELLING HIM WHAT **INGREDIENT** HE NEEDED.
SO THE FIRST CLUE WAS **IRON SOLUTE,** AND THIS ONE IS **TUNGSTEN!**
THAT'S WHAT THIS CONTEST IS ALL ABOUT! WE'RE PUTTING TOGETHER SOME KIND OF **FORMULA!**
LOOKS LIKE WE'RE STILL IN THIS THING.

MEANWHILE...
YOU'RE KILLIN' ME, SALADIN.
MRRRRRRP...
GRACE CAHILL MAY HAVE BEEN A GREAT WOMAN, BUT AS A PET OWNER, SHE CLEARLY DIDN'T KNOW MUCH ABOUT TOUGH LOVE...
THIS IS RIDICULOUS.
AMY AND DAN ARE OUT THERE, RISKING THEIR LIVES FOR CLUES, WHILE WE'RE SITTING HERE TRYING TO FIND YOU THE PERFECT ***FLAVOR PROFILE...***
AND YOU KNOW WHAT? I GIVE UP.
I GUESS I'LL JUST DIP INTO MY SAVINGS TO FUND YOUR RED SNAPPER HABIT.
SPLAT
TOSS
YOU WIN, CAT.
MRRRRRR --

...RRRRP?
SNARF
GOBBLE
SCARF
GOBBLE
SMACK
GOOD BOY, SALADIN! I KNEW YOU'D LOVE IT IF YOU JUST GAVE IT A CHANCE!
IT'S CAT FOOD -- IT'S FOR PEOPLE LIKE YOU!
MYAM
MYAM
MYAM
NELLIE! WE'RE BACK!!

CONGRATULATE ME, YOU GUYS! THE HUNGER STRIKE IS OVER --
WAIT, ARE THOSE SWORDS?!
MYAM MYAM MYAM
PUT THOSE THINGS DOWN BEFORE YOU SLICE YOUR OWN EARS OFF!
IT'S OKAY! THEY'RE THE NEXT CLUE!
SWORDS?
TUNGSTEN!
THAT'S WHAT THE STEEL'S ALLOYED WITH!
MYAM MYAM MYAM
ZING
START PACKING -- WE'RE GOING TO TOKYO!
OH YEAH, AND WAY TO GO, SALADIN! WE KNEW YOU COULD DO IT.
MYAM MYAM MYAM
TOKYO? WHY TOKYO?
THAT'S WHERE THE SWORDS ARE FROM -- AND THE EXHIBIT SAID THAT FIDELIO RACCO WENT OFF TO JAPAN AND WAS NEVER HEARD FROM AGAIN!
THE TRAIL LEADS THERE. THAT'S WHERE WE'LL FIND THE NEXT CLUE.

THE KABRAS HAVE MONEY, THE HOLTS HAVE MUSCLE, IRINA HAS TRAINING, ALISTAIR HAS EXPERIENCE, AND JONAH HAS FAME...
BUT **WE** HAVE THE **SECOND CLUE.**
AND MORE IMPORTANTLY...
WE HAVE **EACH OTHER.**
ALL RIGHT, THEN --
I'LL MAKE A CALL TO JAPAN AIRLINES RIGHT AWAY...
URRRRRP
ON WITH THE CHASE!

SALZBURG, THE NEXT DAY...
MOZART
BE-BEEP
BE-BEEP
BE-BEEP
BE-BEEP
BE-BEEP
ODD...
BE-BEEP
BEEP
MOZART
BEEP
BEEP
BEEP
BEEP
BEEP
BEEP
BEEP
BEEP
BEEP
THAT --
IS THAT WHAT I THINK IT IS?
NO...
SO IT'S *YOU!*

I DON'T APPRECIATE YOUR MEDDLING IN THIS CONTEST!
WHERE IS MY CLUE?
ALISTAIR, I HAVE NOTHING OF YOURS.
THERE WAS A CLUE FROM THE TUNNEL AT ST. PETER'S -- BUT WHEN I WENT TO RETRIEVE IT TO HAVE IT TRANSLATED, I FOUND IT MISSING, AND YOUR HOMING PIN IN THE HEAD OF MY CANE INSTEAD!
SO... YOUR EXPLANATION, IF YOU PLEASE.
I... HAVE NONE.
SO YOU CONFESS THAT YOU'RE TRYING TO INFLUENCE THIS CONTEST... OR PERHAPS YOUR PLAN IS TO HIJACK IT ENTIRELY AND TAKE THE PRIZE FOR YOURSELF!
YOU OUGHT TO KNOW THAT CAHILLS ARE CAPABLE OF ALMOST ANYTHING -- IT COULD HAVE BEEN ANY ONE OF THEM --
BUT I ASSURE YOU, NOT I.
OZART
HMPH. YOU HAVEN'T HEARD THE LAST OF THIS.
WHEN I WIN THE CONTEST, I'LL SEE TO IT THAT YOU NEVER WORK AGAIN!

YOU WON'T BELIEVE IT...
THEY FOUND THE HOMING DEVICE UNDER THE CAT'S COLLAR AND PLANTED IT ON ALISTAIR.
SO WHAT YOU'RE SAYING IS WE'VE **LOST** THE CHILDREN.
IT'S MORE LIKE THE CHILDREN HAVE LOST **US.**
IT WOULD SEEM WE HAVE UNDERESTIMATED THEM...
THEY ARE MORE RESOURCEFUL THAN EVEN MADAME GRACE HAD IMAGINED.

GORDON KORMAN wrote his first novel, *This Can't Be Happening at Macdonald Hall*, when he was thirteen years old. Since then, he's written over a hundred other books, including the #1 *New York Times* bestseller *Restart*, the Sydney Taylor Honor Book *Linked*, *Slacker*, *The Fort*, and *Mixed Up*. He lives on Long Island with his family and can be found online at gordonkorman.com.

HANNAH TEMPLER is an award-winning American cartoonist, best known for her Ignatz-nominated original series *Cosmoknights*, as well as the Eisner Award–winning graphic novel *Flung Out of Space*, which was named a *New York Times* Notable Book of 2022. She has also worked as an artist on numerous titles such as *GLOW*, *Doctor Who*, *TMNT*, *Buffy The Vampire Slayer*, *Samurai Jack*, *Jem and the Holograms*, *Captain Marvel*, and *Tomb Raider*. You can find her online at hannahtempler.com.